Vivaldi Violin Concertos
A Handbook

by

Arlan Stone Martin

The Scarecrow Press, Inc.
Metuchen, N.J. 1972

ISBN 0-8108-0432-8

Library of Congress Catalog Card Number 76-169698

DEDICATION

To Antonio Vivaldi

CONTENTS

INTRODUCTION

One wonders why the works of a composer of the stature of Antonio Vivaldi are so unjustly neglected. This applies to his violin concertos in particular. The most important reason for this neglect is the fact that much of his music has only recently become available to the performing musician.

Now that the recording and publishing companies are beginning to show an interest in the works of Vivaldi, there has been a greater interest on the part of the listener and the performer as well, to acquire various recordings and sheet music of his compositions.

A new problem then arises. The cataloging system has not been standardized for Vivaldi's compositions, making it difficult to locate and identify any single work. The need exists for a handbook listing all the available index numbers for a given work to simplify the identification process. The present Handbook seeks to serve that need, organizing all the pertinent identification data for the Vivaldi violin concertos into a useful form.

There are four different indexes in use at the present time which contain lists of the Vivaldi violin concertos. These are:

1. Rinaldi Catalogo -- lists by opus number with incipit. [Mario Rinaldi, Numerico Tematico dello Composizioni di Antonio Vivaldi (Italy: Editrice Culture Moderna, 1945).]

2. Pincherle Inventaire Thèmatique -- lists instrumental works with major and relative minor keys grouped together. [Marc Pincherle, Antonio Vivaldi et la Musique Instrumentale, Tome 2, Inventaire Thèmatique (Paris: Librarie Floury, 1948).]

3. Coral Concordance -- contains the old Pincherle numbering system plus a partial cross index with the Fanna

numbers of Ricordi and the opus numbers of Rinaldi. [Lenore Coral, A Concordance of the Thematic Indexes to the Instrumental Works of Antonio Vivaldi (Ann Arbor: Music Library Association Publications, 1965).]

4. Ricordi Catalogo -- lists by order of key with incipit and Fanna numbers. [Ricordi Instituto Italiano Antonio Vivaldi, Catalogo Numerico-Tematico delle Opere Strumentale (Italy: G. Ricordi, 1968).]

Unfortunately none of these four indexes gives a complete cross-index to the others. Since music publishers as well as recording companies do not have any one set list of numbers to follow when listing works of Vivaldi, the result has been a haphazard listing of the violin concertos, making it extremely difficult to identify any one concerto unless it has a particular title to it. Considering Vivaldi wrote over 238 violin concertos, one can see the difficulty of attempting to identify or locate any particular concerto.

Lenore Coral in the Preface to her Concordance states:

> Perhaps when Fanna releases the complete catalog which is intended to accompany the Ricordi Edition,[1] the Pincherle index will be superseded.[2]

This hope has not been fulfilled. It is hard to persuade others to discard the older and less accurate systems of listing. The Library of Congress still lists the works of Vivaldi by Rinaldi opus numbers, which means libraries which use the Library of Congress classification will all catalog Vivaldi concertos with the old Rinaldi numbers. The publishers and recording companies are still using a mixed listing for Vivaldi concertos. They usually list by key and add an identifying number or name from one of the previously listed indexes if they happen to have it. Therefore it is obvious a new type of catalog for these works is needed, which should be a composite of all available listings relating to the violin concertos of Antonio Vivaldi.

This Handbook will be limited to listing only those 238 violin concertos of Antonio Vivaldi which are listed in the Ricordi Catalogo.[3] Included in this listing will be those concertos for more than one violin soloist with orchestra.

The listing of published music and recorded works

will be limited to those concertos given in Farish's *String Music in Print,*[4] its *Supplement,*[5] the Schwann *Monthly Guide to Stereo Records*[6] from 1949-1970, and whatever available literature it is possible to obtain from the various publishing companies.

The Handbook will be based on the four catalogs previously listed which are used so extensively today. Therefore a short summary of the information found in each catalog would be helpful to the reader.

The Rinaldi catalog lists all of the works composed by Vivaldi which were available to the editor at the time of publication. The works are listed according to opus numbers from opus 1 to opus 319. Vivaldi never put any dates on his manuscripts, but in his lifetime he did send to the publishers various groups of works which he listed under opus numbers. These included those works which are known as opus 1 to opus 14. He united those compositions under one opus number which he felt were compatible. The grouping was done by type of instrument, musical ensemble, or form. The Rinaldi catalog has tried to follow this type of grouping in listing all other works of Vivaldi. A thematic listing along with the names of movements is given for each work with its opus number. Duplications of some concertos do exist. This may be due to the fact that more than one manuscript or edition was found for an individual work, and these were inadvertantly listed under new opus numbers.

The Pincherle *Inventaire Thèmatique* is the second volume to *Antonio Vivaldi et la Musique Instrumentale.*[7] It contains two classifications of Vivaldi's compositions. The first classification lists work in published collections. The second lists all works (published and in manuscript) by tonality in major and relative minor groupings.

The Coral *Concordance* uses the Pincherle system as the main basis of numbering the works of Vivaldi. She groups the compositions by units (each major key with its relative minor) as Pincherle did. This random grouping of major and minor keys as a unit makes it impossible to identify any particular concerto in her *Concordance* by specific key since a thematic index is not given. The main advantage to her *Concordance* is in the fact that she has cross-indexed the Pincherle numbers with the Rinaldi opus numbers, and with the Fanna numbers of Ricordi up to Fanna I, no. 172. She did not list the higher Fanna numbers since they were not available at the time her book was published.

Ricordi's catalog groups all compositions by instrument and by type of composition. All violin concertos are listed under the number Fanna I. There are 236 concertos for violin among the instrumental works of Vivaldi listed in this catalog. Two additional violin concertos are listed in a supplementary section in the back of the book, which lists works of Vivaldi which were discovered after the catalog had been finished. The compositions in the Ricordi catalog are listed by order of key and the relating incipits are given with the Fanna number and Ricordi fascicle number. The keys are listed starting with C Major in chromatic scale order. Four appendices are given at the end of the thematic index:

1. Appendix I lists by the Fanna numbering system.

2. Appendix II lists the Ricordi fascicle numbers as well as the general catalog number of the Ricordi published editions of music.

3. Appendix III lists the opus numbers from opus 1 to opus 14 as they were published in Vivaldi's lifetime.

4. Appendix IV gives the Pincherle list in numerical order with the matching Fanna numbers.

The Ricordi catalog lists only those concertos definitely attributed to Vivaldi. It does not include unfinished manuscripts, inaccessible manuscripts, or lost ones.

Organization of This Handbook

This Handbook will give all the available catalog numbers, and titles if any, for each individual concerto in one place, listing each violin concerto by order of key along with the relating incipits for that particular work. There will be further notations underneath the incipits stating whether this work has been published or recorded, and the names of the companies supplying those scores and records will be given along with the series numbers for ordering purposes.

A short cross-index for all the catalogs will precede this detailed incipit guide. It will be listed by order of the

Fanna numbers of Ricordi, giving specific keys and identifying features of the works. This short cross-index will save valuable time for the researcher who needs a quick reference to any violin concerto and its accompanying data.

Five appendices will be given to this Handbook:

A. The first appendix will list concertos by their order of key in chromatic scale order, giving the Handbook page number in the incipit guide (i.e., Chapter II) where concertos of a particular key will begin their listing.

B. The second appendix will list concertos by Fanna numbers, and will then also refer to the Handbook page where the incipit for each Fanna number is given.

C. The third appendix will use the Pincherle numbering system, referring back again to the page number in this Handbook for the relevant incipit.

D. The fourth appendix will list the concertos in order of their Rinaldi opus numbers, also then giving the Handbook page number where each concerto incipit may be located.

E. The last appendix will list collections of Vivaldi violin concerto recordings. Those recordings which are listed in the incipit guide (Chapter II) are only for individual concertos, and do not include those recordings of works in collected editions. The reader would be wise to check both lists of recordings since some concertos will have listings in both places.

Any person who has ever attempted to locate any one concerto will now be able not only to identify the themes but also to find the printed score in the Ricordi collected volumes of Vivaldi's instrumental works located in the larger music libraries, and will know how to order any one of the published concertos from the publisher printing that particular work, or the recording company which has recorded it. Let us hope that in making these concertos more readily available to the general public, there will be a renewed interest in playing more of these beautiful, but neglected works. It is a pity that too often these concertos have been left on library shelves in reference collections because the knowledge of where to secure the music has not been known.

Notes

1. Antonio Vivaldi, Le Opere di Antonio Vivaldi (Rome: Edizioni Ricordi, 1947-).

2. Coral, Concordance, p. 3.

3. Ricordi Istituto Italiano Antonio Vivaldi, Catalogo Numerico-Tematico delle Opere Strumentale (Italy: G. Ricordi & Co., 1968).

4. Margaret K. Farish, String Music in Print (New York: R.R. Bowker, 1965).

5. Margaret K. Farish, Supplement to String Music in Print (New York: R.R. Bowker, 1968).

6. Long Playing Record Catalog (Monthly Guide to Stereo Records) (Boston: W. Schwann, 1949 to 1970).

7. Marc Pincherle, Antonio Vivaldi et la Musique Instrumentale (Paris: Librarie Floury, 1948).

Chapter I

A SHORT CROSS-INDEX

Fanna (1)	Ricordi (Tomo)	Pincherle	Rinaldi (Opus)	Key (& Identifying Features)
1	1	405	33, No. 8	B♭ Major
2	4	419	51, No. 3	c minor ("Il Sospetto")
3	13	88	56, No. 7	C Major
4	15	248	51, No. 2	E Major ("Il Riposo")
5	16	236	31, No. 5 56, No. 6	A Major
6	27	132	21, No. 1	G Major (for 2 violins)
7	29	244	33, No. 14	E Major
8	31	199	38, No. 5	D Major
9	38	429	33, No. 1	E♭ Major
10	37	208	51, No. 1	D Major ("L' Inquietudine")
11	45	310	20, No. 1	d minor (scordatura [3d movt.])
12	48	436	21, No. 4	c minor (for 2 violins)
13	55	14	54, No. 3	C Major ("Per la S. S. Assunzione di Maria Vergine")
14	60	435	21, No. 2	c minor (for 2 violins)
15	64	409	56, No. 5	B♭ Major
16	65	337	36, No. 1 (8, No. 8)	g minor
17	66	324	56, No. 1	F Major
18	68	200	36, No. 4	D Major
19	69	201	36, No. 6	D Major

Fanna (I)	Ricordi (Tomo)	Pincherle	Rinaldi (Opus)	Key (& Identifying Features)
20	70	290	31, No. 2	F Major ("per la Solennita di San Lorenzo")
21	74	316	36, No. 3	d minor
22	76	241	8, No. 1	E Major ("La Primavera")
23	77	336	8, No. 2	g minor ("L' Estate")
24	78	257	8, No. 3	F Major (L' Autunno")
25	79	442	8, No. 4	f minor ("L' Inverno")
26	80	415	8, No. 5	E♭ Major ("La Tempesta di Mare")
27	81	7	8, No. 6	C Major ("Il Piacere")
28	82	258	8, No. 7	d minor (per Pisendel)
29	83	338	8, No. 10	B♭ Major ("La Caccia")
30	84	153	8, No. 11 (36, No. 12)	D Major
31	85	8	8, No. 12	C Major
32	86	373	31, No. 12	B♭ Major
33	87	325	56, No. 3	F Major
34	88	278	23, No. 1 (61, No. 20)	F Major (for 3 violins)
35	89	190	21, No. 8	D Major (for 2 violins)
36	92	408	56, No. 2	g minor
37	93	144	56, No. 4	e minor
38	96	184	33, No. 6	b minor
39	100	229	20, No. 2	A Major (scordatura)
40	107	390	21, No. 5	B♭ Major (for 2 violins)
41	108	189	21, No. 7	D Major (for 2 violins)

Fanna (I)	Ricordi (Tomo)	Pincherle	Rinaldi (Opus)	Key (& Identifying Features)
42	111	391	21, No. 6	B♭ Major (for 2 violins)
43	112	23	58, No. 1 (61, No. 13)	C Major (for 2 violins)
44	116	17	21, No. 9	C Major (for 2 violins)
45	117	171	36, No. 2	D Major
46	120	59	35, No. 1	C Major
47	122	9	35, No. 7 (9, No. 1	C Major (last movt. 35, No. 7 differs)
48	123	242	9, No. 4 (31, No. 17)	E Major (last movt. 31, No. 17 differs)
49	124	103	9, No. 10	G Major
50	125	154	9, No. 12	b minor (scordatura)
51	126	214	9, No. 2	A Major
52	127	339	9, No. 3 (11, No. 6)	g minor
53	128	10	9, No. 5 (61, No. 19)	a minor
54	129	215	9, No. 6	A Major (scordatura)
55	130	340	9, No. 7	B♭ Major
56	131	260	9, No. 8	d minor
57	132	341	9, No. 9	B♭ Major (for 2 violins)
58	133	416	9, No. 11 (61, No. 15)	c minor
59	134	367	27, No. 5	B♭ Major (for 4 violins)
60	136	368	28, No. 3	B♭ Major (scordatura) (for violin & 2 orchestras)
61	140	28	58, No. 2	a minor (for 2 violins)
62	141	164	54, No. 2	D Major ("Per la S. S. Assunzione di Maria Vergine")

Fanna (I)	Ricordi (Tomo)	Pincherle	Rinaldi (Opus)	Key (& Identifying Features)
63	145	389	21, No. 3	B♭ Major (for 2 violins)
64	156	138	47, No. 1	G Major
65	157	356	33, No. 4	B♭ Major
66	158	295	33, No. 3	F Major
67	160	21	33, No. 2	C Major
68	162	20S (S=Sinfonia)	32, No. 2	C Major (for 2 violins)
69	163	376	33, No. 5	B♭ Major
70	164	125	33, No. 7	e minor
71	165	296	33, No. 9	F Major
72	166	245	33, No. 10	E Major
73	167	40	33, No. 11	C Major
74	168	126	33, No. 13	e minor
75	169	430	33, No. 16	E♭ Major
76	170	377	33, No. 15	B♭ Major
77	171	185	33, No. 12	b minor
78	172	378	33, No. 18	B♭ Major
79	173	431	33, No. 20	c minor
80	174	186	33, No. 17	D Major
81	175	379	33, No. 19	g minor
82	178	357	36, No. 5	g minor
83	179	202	36, No. 7	b minor
84	180	247	36, No. 13	E Major
85	181	65	37, No. 1	C Major (for 2 violins)
86	183	344	12, No. 5 (36, No. 9)	B♭ Major
87	186	136	36, No. 16	G Major
88	187	317	36, No. 8	F Major
89	188	156	36, No. 10 (11, No. 1)	D Major
90	191	216	11, No. 3 (36, No. 18)	A Major
91	192	111	36, No. 17 (61, No. 7)	G Major (per Pisendel)
92	193	439	36, No. 20	E♭ Major
93	194	66	36, No. 15	C Major

Fanna (I)	Ricordi (Tomo)	Pincherle	Rinaldi (Opus)	Key (& Identifying Features)
94	195	68	36, No. 19	C Major
95	199	349	36, No. 11	B♭Major
96	202	117	28, No. 1	G Major
97	203	179	28, No. 2	D Major
98	207	366	27, No. 2	g minor (for 2 violins)
99	208	365	27, No. 1	B♭Major (for 2 violins)
100	209	281	27, No. 3	d minor (for 2 violins)
101	210	423	27, No. 4	E♭Major (for 2 violins)
102	227	425	31, No. 6	E♭Major
103	228	121	31, No. 4	G Major
104	229	237	31, No. 7	A Major
105	230	426	31, No. 8	c minor
106	245	234	31, No. 3	A Major
107	247	122	31, No. 9	G Major
108	253	372	31, No. 10	g minor
109	254	428	31, No. 21	E♭Major
110	255	124	31, No. 11	G Major
111	256	38	31, No. 13	C Major
112	257	374	31, No. 14	g minor
113	258	293	31, No. 16	d minor
114	259	39	31, No. 20	C Major
115	260	183	31, No. 18	b minor
116	261	182	31, No. 15	D Major
117	262	375	31, No. 19	B♭Major
118	284	370	31, No. 1	B♭Major
119	285	272	35, No. 4	d minor
120	286	193	35, No. 8	D Major
121	291	396	35, No. 12	B♭Major
122	292	395	35, No. 10	g minor
123	293	225	35, No. 11	A Major
124	294	192	35, No. 3	D Major
125	295	393	35, No. 2	g minor
126	296	312	35, No. 5	d minor

Fanna (I)	Ricordi (Tomo)	Pincherle	Rinaldi (Opus)	Key (& Identifying Features)
127	297	246	35, No. 6	E Major ("L'Amoroso")
128	301	314	35, No. 15	F Major
129	302	170	35, No. 14 (61, No. 17)	D Major
130	303	315	35, No. 17	F Major
131	304	437	35, No. 18	E♭ Major
132	305	194	35, No. 21	D Major
133	306	195	35, No. 22	D Major
134	307	196	35, No. 23	D Major
135	311	62	35, No. 16	C Major
136	312	165	35, No. 19	D Major
137	313	239	35, No. 20	A Major
138	314	151	35, No. 13	D Major
139	319	222	62, No. 2	A Major (per l ' "eco in lontano")
140	322	19	61, No. 1	C Major
141	323	228		A Major
142	324	269	61, No. 3	d minor
143	325	277	61, No. 2	d minor
144	326	168	61, No. 10	b minor
145	327	243		E Major
146	328	22		C Major
147	329	352		g minor
148	330	227		A Major
149	331	173		D Major
150	332	358		B♭ Major
151	333	276		d minor
152	334	354	61, No. 18	g minor
153	335	167		D Major
154	336	270	61, No. 9	d minor
155	339	223		A Major
156	340	420	61, No. 11	E♭ Major
157	342	18		C Major (for 2 violins)
158	343	161	61, No. 4	D Major
159	344	224	62, No. 1	A Major (for 2 violins)

Fanna (I)	Ricordi (Tomo)	Pincherle	Rinaldi (Opus)	Key (& Identifying Features)
160	345	162	61, No. 5	D Major
161	346	275	61, No. 16	F Major
162	347	163	61, No. 6	D Major
163	348	350		B♭ Major ("O sia Corneto da posta")
164	349	418		E♭ Major
165	351	351	64, No. 3	g minor
166	352	421	61, No. 14	E♭ Major
167	357	271		F Major
168	358	112		G Major
169	376	29		C Major
170	377	353		B♭ Major
171	378	172		b minor
172	379	20	61, No. 8	C Major
173	408	96	3, No. 3	G Major
174	409	97	3, No. 4	e minor (for 4 violins)
175	410	212	3, No. 5	A Major (for 2 violins)
176	411	1	3, No. 6	a minor
177	413	2	3, No. 8	a minor (for 2 violins)
178	414	147	3, No. 9	D Major
179	417	240	3, No. 12	E Major
180	418	327	4, No. 1	B♭ Major (same 1st movt. as Fanna I 235)
181	419	98	4, No. 2	e minor
182	420	99	4, No. 3	G Major
183	421	3	4, No. 4	a minor
184	422	213	4, No. 5	A Major
185	423	328	4, No. 6	g minor
186	424	4	4, No. 7	C Major
187	425	253	4, No. 8	d minor
188	426	251	4, No. 9	F Major
189	427	413	4, No. 10	c minor
190	428	149	4, No. 11	D Major

Fanna (I)	Ricordi (Tomo)	Pincherle	Rinaldi (Opus)	Key (& Identifying Features)
191	429	100	4, No. 12	G Major
192	436	329	6, No. 1	g minor
193	414 355	437	6, No. 2	E♭Major
194	438	330	6, No. 3	g minor
195	439	150	6, No. 4	D Major
196	440	101	6, No. 5	e minor
197	441	254	6, No. 6	d minor
198	443	5	7, No. 2	C Major
199	444	332	7, No. 3	g minor
200	445	6	7, No. 4	a minor
201	446	255	7, No. 5	F Major
202	447	333	7, No. 6	B♭Major
203	449	102	7, No. 8	G Major
204	450	335	7, No. 9	B♭Major
205	451	256	7, No. 10 (61, No. 12)	F Major
206	452	151	7, No. 11	D Major
207	453	152	7, No. 12	D Major
208	459	106	11, No. 2	e minor ("Il Favorito")
209	460	107	11, No. 4	G Major
210	461	417	11, No. 5	c minor
211	462	343	12, No. 1	g minor
212	463	263	12, No. 2	d minor
213	465	11	12, No. 4	C Major
214	466	345	12, No. 6	B♭Major
215	479	252		F Major
216	480	108		e minor
217	481	12		C Major
218	482	158		D Major
219	483	346	16, No. 1	B♭Major
220	484	109	16, No. 2	e minor
221	485	217		A Major
222	486	159		D Major (for 2 violins)
223	487	219		A Major
224	489	221	Op. 66	A Major
225	494	174		D Major

Fanna (I)	Ricordi (Tomo)	Pincherle	Rinaldi (Opus)	Key (& Identifying Features)
226	495			C Major
227	496	232		A Major
228	497	177		D Major
229	498	178		b minor
230	499	364		B♭ Major
231	502			E♭ Major ("Il Ritiro")
232	508	93		C Major
233	511	412		B♭ Major
234	513	211		D Major
235	514	327	4, No. 1	B♭ Major (Same 1st movt. as Fanna I 180)
236	519	92		a minor
237				D Major
238				e minor

Chapter II

INCIPIT GUIDE

Begin: Concertos in C Major for Violin

Fanna I	Ricordi (Tomo)	Pincherle	Rinaldi
3	13	88	Op. 56, No. 7

PUBLICATIONS

Violin & Orchestra

Editor	Publisher	Series No.
Moderna	G. Ricordi & Co.	PR 249

RECORDINGS

Label	Series No.
Angel	S-36001

C MAJOR

"Per la S.S. Assunzione di Maria Vergine"

Fanna I	Ricordi (Tomo)	Pincherle	Rinaldi
13	55	14	Op. 54, No. 3

PUBLICATIONS

Violin & Orchestra

Editor	Publisher	Series No.
Moderna	G. Ricordi & Co.	PR 342

Violin & Piano

Editor	Publisher	Series No.
Bellezza	G. Ricordi & Co.	129590

RECORDINGS

Label	Series No.
Seraphim	S-60118

C MAJOR

"Il Piacere"

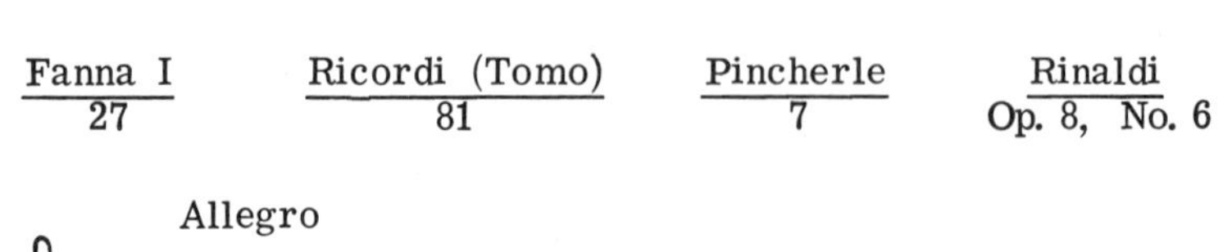

Fanna I	Ricordi (Tomo)	Pincherle	Rinaldi
27	81	7	Op. 8, No. 6

Allegro

Largo e cantabile

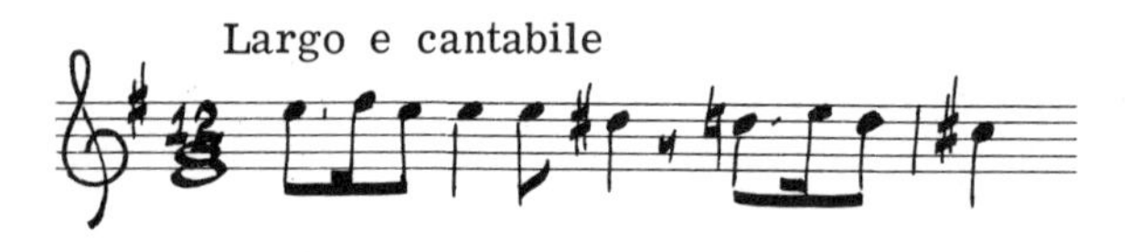

Allegro

PUBLICATIONS

Violin & Orchestra

Editor	Publisher	Series No.
Malipiero	G. Ricordi & Co.	PR 443

RECORDINGS*

Label	Series No.
Epic	LC-3343

*See Appendix E

C MAJOR

Fanna I	Ricordi (Tomo)	Pincherle	Rinaldi
31	85	8	Op. 8, No. 12

PUBLICATIONS

Violin & Orchestra

Editor	Publisher	Series No.
Malipiero	G. Ricordi & Co.	PR 448

RECORDINGS*

*See Appendix E

C MAJOR

Concerto for 2 Violins

Fanna I	Ricordi (Tomo)	Pincherle	Rinaldi
43	112	23	Op. 58, No. 1 (Op. 61, No. 13)

PUBLICATIONS

Violin & Orchestra

Editor	Publisher	Series No.
Malipiero	G. Ricordi & Co.	PR 562

C MAJOR

Concerto for 2 Violins

Fanna I	Ricordi (Tomo)	Pincherle	Rinaldi
44	116	17	Op. 21, No. 9

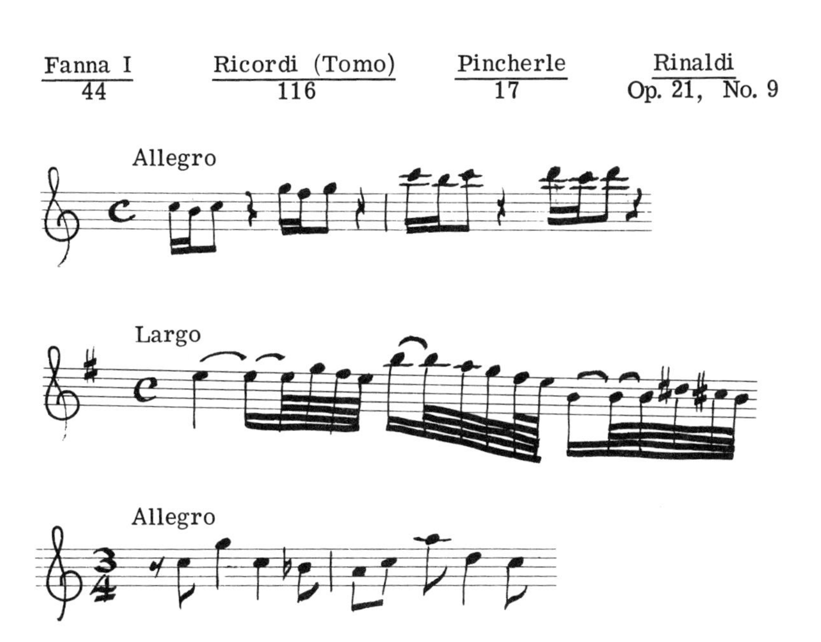

PUBLICATIONS

Violin & Orchestra

Editor	Publisher	Series No.
Malipiero	G. Ricordi & Co.	PR 566

C MAJOR

Fanna I	Ricordi (Tomo)	Pincherle	Rinaldi
46	120	59	Op. 35, No. 1

PUBLICATIONS

Violin & Orchestra

Editor	Publisher	Series No.
Malipiero	G. Ricordi & Co.	PR 570

C MAJOR

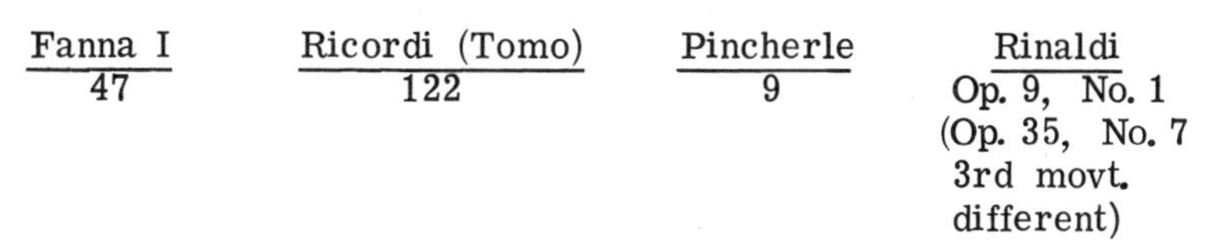

Fanna I	Ricordi (Tomo)	Pincherle	Rinaldi
47	122	9	Op. 9, No. 1 (Op. 35, No. 7 3rd movt. different)

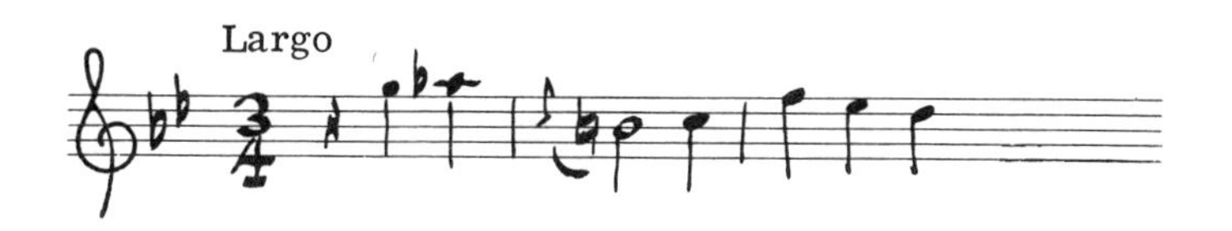

PUBLICATIONS

Violin & Orchestra

Editor	Publisher	Series No.
Malipiero	G. Ricordi & Co.	PR 572

RECORDINGS*

*See Appendix E

C MAJOR

Fanna I	Ricordi (Tomo)	Pincherle	Rinaldi
67	160	21	Op. 33, No. 2

PUBLICATIONS

Violin & Orchestra

Editor	Publisher	Series No.
Malipiero	G. Ricordi & Co.	PR 685

C MAJOR

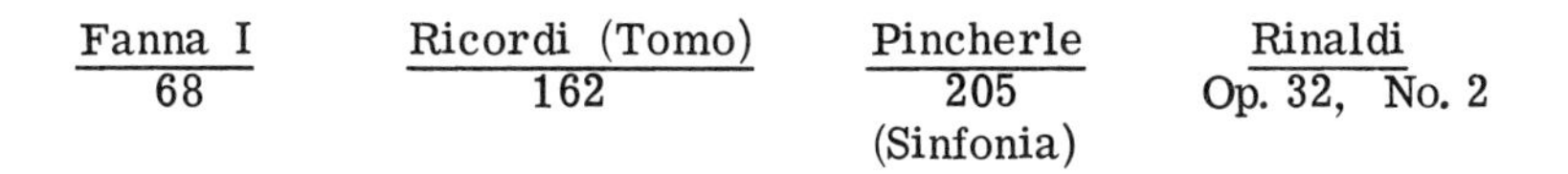

Fanna I	Ricordi (Tomo)	Pincherle	Rinaldi
68	162	205 (Sinfonia)	Op. 32, No. 2

Optional 3rd movement:

PUBLICATIONS

Violin & Orchestra

Editor	Publisher	Series No.
Malipiero	G. Ricordi & Co.	PR 687

C MAJOR

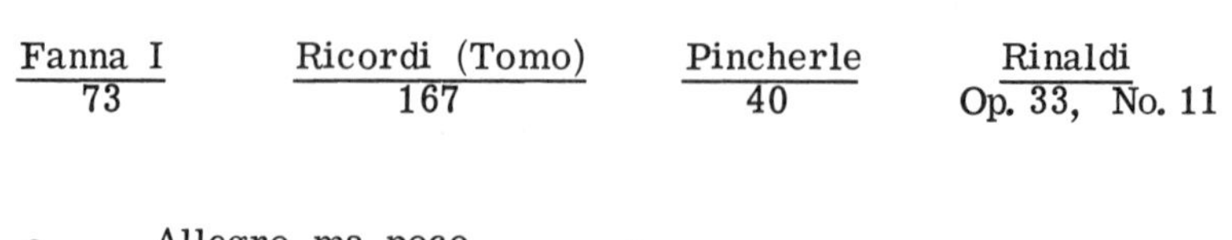

Fanna I	Ricordi (Tomo)	Pincherle	Rinaldi
73	167	40	Op. 33, No. 11

PUBLICATIONS

Violin & Orchestra

Editor	Publisher	Series No.
Malipiero	G. Ricordi & Co.	PR 692

C MAJOR

Concerto for 2 Violins

Fanna I	Ricordi (Tomo)	Pincherle	Rinaldi
85	181	65	Op. 37, No. 1

PUBLICATIONS

Violin & Orchestra

Editor	Publisher	Series No.
Malipiero	G. Ricordi & Co.	PR 706

C MAJOR

Fanna I	Ricordi (Tomo)	Pincherle	Rinaldi
93	194	66	Op. 36, No. 15

PUBLICATIONS

Violin & Orchestra

Editor	Publisher	Series No.
Malipiero	G. Ricordi & Co.	PR 719

C MAJOR

Fanna I	Ricordi (Tomo)	Pincherle	Rinaldi
94	195	68	Op. 36, No. 19

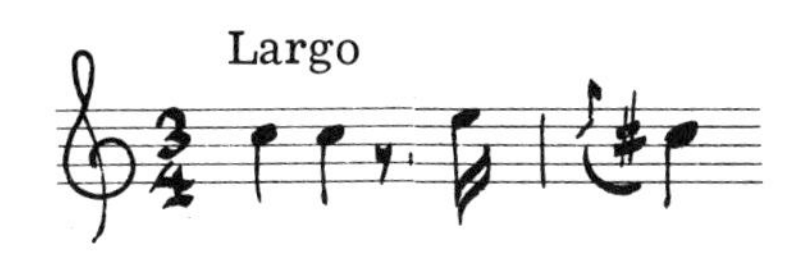

PUBLICATIONS

Violin & Orchestra

Editor	Publisher	Series No.
Malipiero	G. Ricordi & Co.	PR 270

C MAJOR

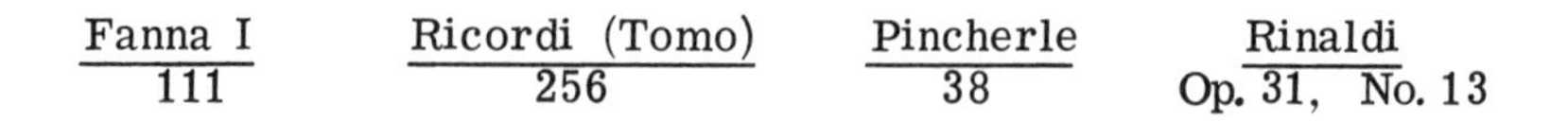

Fanna I	Ricordi (Tomo)	Pincherle	Rinaldi
111	256	38	Op. 31, No. 13

PUBLICATIONS

Violin & Orchestra

Editor	Publisher	Series No.
Malipiero	G. Ricordi & Co.	PR 881

C MAJOR

Fanna I	Ricordi (Tomo)	Pincherle	Rinaldi
114	259	39	Op. 31, No. 20

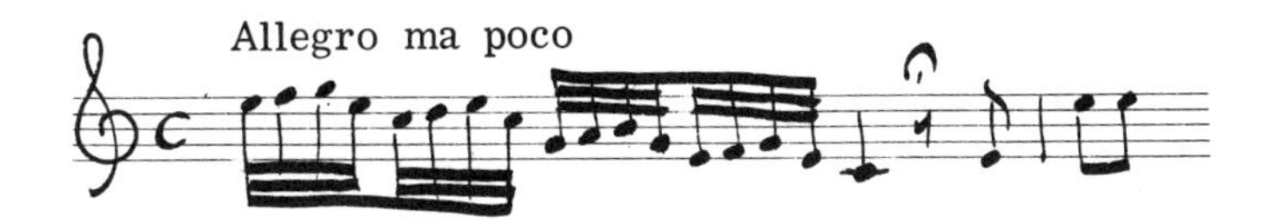

Allegro ma poco

PUBLICATIONS

Violin & Orchestra

Editor	Publisher	Series No.
Malipiero	G. Ricordi & Co.	PR 884

C MAJOR

Fanna I	Ricordi (Tomo)	Pincherle	Rinaldi
135	311	62	Op. 35, No. 16

PUBLICATIONS

Violin & Orchestra

Editor	Publisher	Series No.
Malipiero	G. Ricordi & Co.	PR 961

C MAJOR

Fanna I	Ricordi (Tomo)	Pincherle	Rinaldi
140	332	19	Op. 61, No. 1

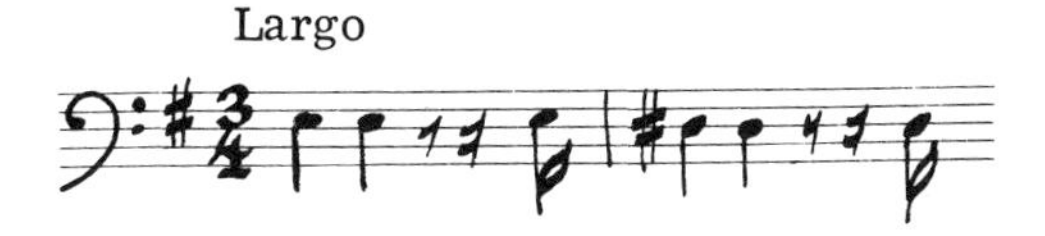

PUBLICATIONS

Violin & Orchestra

Editor	Publisher	Series No.
Malipiero	G. Ricordi & Co.	PR 972

C MAJOR

Fanna I	Ricordi (Tomo)	Pincherle	Rinaldi
146	328	22	

PUBLICATIONS

Violin & Orchestra

Editor	Publisher	Series No.
Malipiero	G. Ricordi & Co.	PR 978

C MAJOR

Concerto for 2 Violins

Fanna I	Ricordi (Tomo)	Pincherle	Rinaldi
157	342	18	

PUBLICATIONS

Violin & Orchestra

Editor	Publisher	Series No.
Malipiero	G. Ricordi & Co.	PR 992

C MAJOR

Fanna I	Ricordi (Tomo)	Pincherle	Rinaldi
169	376	29	

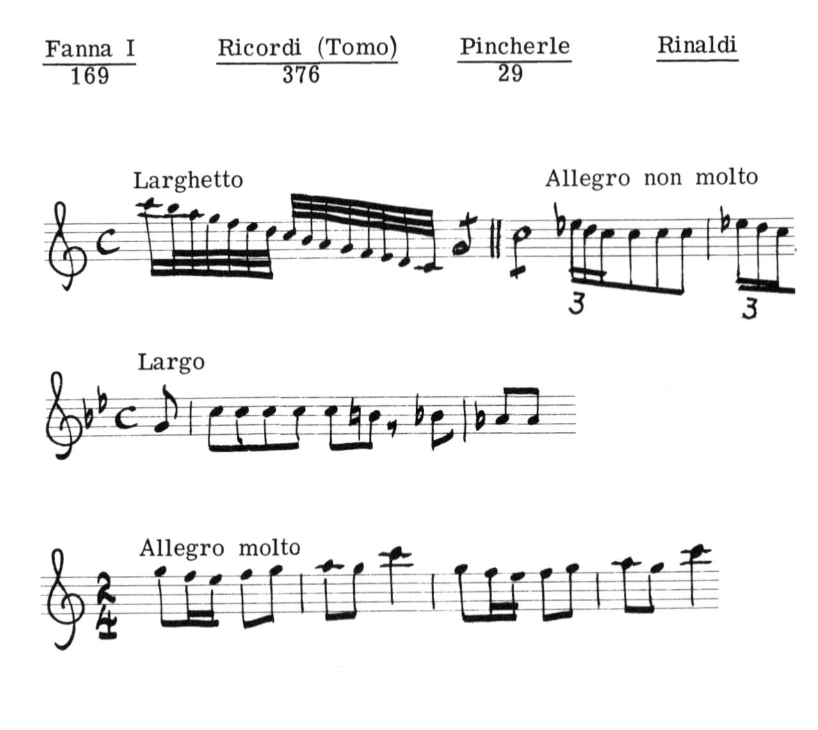

PUBLICATIONS

Violin & Orchestra

Editor	Publisher	Series No.
Malipiero	G. Ricordi & Co.	PR 1051

C MAJOR

Fanna I	Ricordi (Tomo)	Pincherle	Rinaldi
172	379	20	Op. 61, No. 8

PUBLICATIONS

Violin & Orchestra

Editor	Publisher	Series No.
Malipiero	G. Ricordi & Co.	PR 1054

C MAJOR

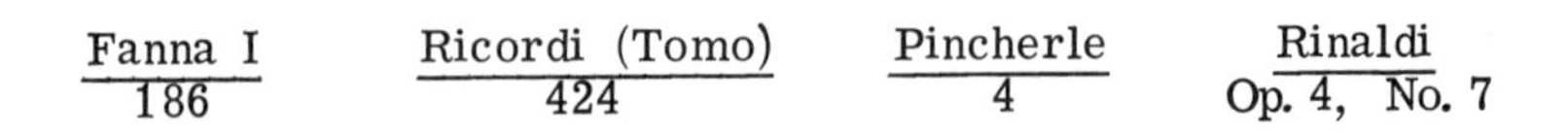

Fanna I	Ricordi (Tomo)	Pincherle	Rinaldi
186	424	4	Op. 4, No. 7

PUBLICATIONS

Violin & Orchestra

Editor	Publisher	Series No.
Ephrikian	G. Ricordi & Co.	PR 1099

RECORDINGS*

*See Appendix E

C MAJOR

Fanna I	Ricordi (Tomo)	Pincherle	Rinaldi
198	443	5	Op. 7, No. 2

PUBLICATIONS

Violin & Orchestra

Editor	Publisher	Series No.
Malipiero	G. Ricordi & Co.	PR 1118

C MAJOR

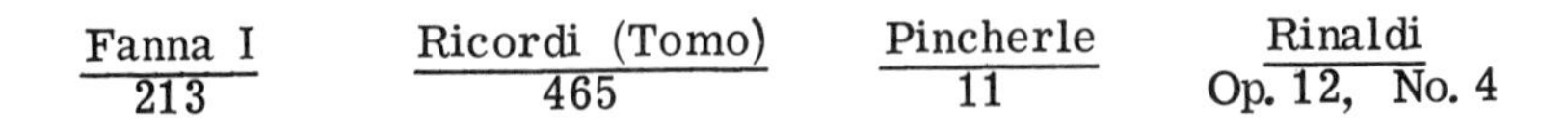

Fanna I	Ricordi (Tomo)	Pincherle	Rinaldi
213	465	11	Op. 12, No. 4

PUBLICATIONS

Violin & Orchestra

Editor	Publisher	Series No.
Ephrikian	G. Ricordi & Co.	PR 1140

C MAJOR

Fanna I	Ricordi (Tomo)	Pincherle	Rinaldi
217	481	12	

C MAJOR

Fanna I	Ricordi (Tomo)	Pincherle	Rinaldi
226	495		

C MAJOR

Fanna I	Ricordi (Tomo)	Pincherle	Rinaldi
232	508	93	

Begin: Concertos in C Minor

"Il Sospetto"

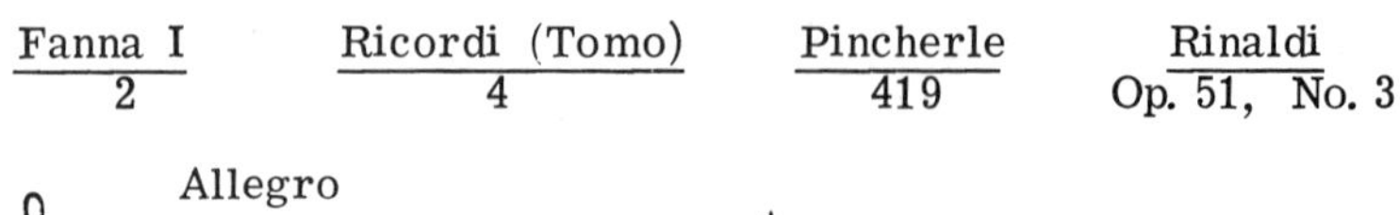

Fanna I	Ricordi (Tomo)	Pincherle	Rinaldi
2	4	419	Op. 51, No. 3

PUBLICATIONS

Violin & Orchestra

Editor	Publisher	Series No.
Ephrikian	G. Ricordi & Co.	PR 233
	C. F. Peters Corp.	

Violin & Piano

Editor	Publisher	Series No.
Glenn	G. Ricordi & Co.	129156
Hin	C. F. Peters Corp.	H-2001

RECORDINGS

Label	Series No.	Label	Series No.
Angel	36001;S-36001	Epic	BC-1021
Baroque	1832-2832	Epic	LC-3486
Decca	9729	Period	514

C MINOR

Concerto for 2 Violins

Fanna I	Ricordi (Tomo)	Pincherle	Rinaldi
12	48	436	Op. 21, No. 4

PUBLICATIONS

Violin & Orchestra

Editor	Publisher	Series No.
Olivieri	G. Ricordi & Co.	PR 315

Violin & Piano

Editor	Publisher	Series No.
	International Music Co.	

RECORDINGS

Label	Series No.
Columbia	ML-5604; MS-6204

C MINOR

Concerto for 2 Violins

Fanna I	Ricordi (Tomo)	Pincherle	Rinaldi
14	60	435	Op. 21, No. 2

PUBLICATIONS

Violin & Orchestra

Editor	Publisher	Series No.
Malipiero	G. Ricordi & Co.	PR 347

C MINOR

Fanna I	Ricordi (Tomo)	Pincherle	Rinaldi
58	133	416	Op. 9, No. 11 (Op. 61, No. 15)

PUBLICATIONS

Violin & Orchestra

Editor	Publisher	Series No.
Malipiero	G. Ricordi & Co. C. F. Peters Corp.	PR 583

RECORDINGS*

*See Appendix E

C MINOR

Fanna I	Ricordi (Tomo)	Pincherle	Rinaldi
79	173	431	Op. 33, No. 20

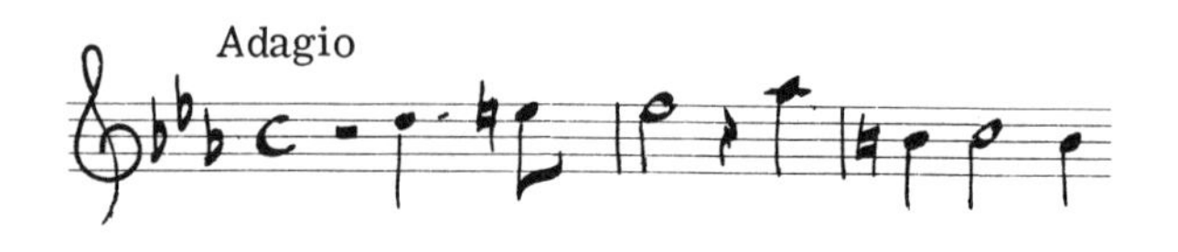

PUBLICATIONS

Violin & Orchestra

Editor	Publisher	Series No.
Malipiero	G. Ricordi & Co.	PR 698

C MINOR

Fanna I	Ricordi (Tomo)	Pincherle	Rinaldi
105	230	426	Op. 31, No. 8

PUBLICATIONS

Violin & Orchestra

Editor	Publisher	Series No.
Ephrikian	G. Ricordi & Co.	PR 830

C MINOR

Fanna I	Ricordi (Tomo)	Pincherle	Rinaldi
189	427	413	Op. 4, No. 10

PUBLICATIONS

Violin & Orchestra

Editor	Publisher	Series No.
Ephrikian	G. Ricordi & Co.	PR 1102

RECORDINGS*

*See Appendix E

C MINOR

Fanna I	Ricordi (Tomo)	Pincherle	Rinaldi
210	461	417	Op. 11, No. 5

PUBLICATIONS

Violin & Orchestra

Editor	Publisher	Series No.
Malipiero	G. Ricordi & Co.	PR 1136

Violin & Piano

Editor	Publisher	Series No.
Abbado	G. Ricordi & Co.	130165

Begin: Concertos in D Major

Fanna I	Ricordi (Tomo)	Pincherle	Rinaldi
8	31	199	Op. 38, No. 5

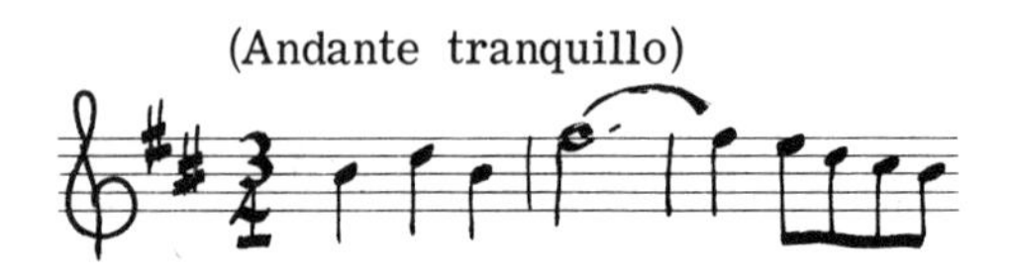

PUBLICATIONS

Violin & Orchestra

Editor	Publisher	Series No.
Maderna	G. Ricordi & Co.	PR 289

D MAJOR

"L'Inquietudine"

Fanna I	Ricordi (Tomo)	Pincherle	Rinaldi
10	37	208	Op. 51, No. 1

PUBLICATIONS

Violin & Orchestra

Editor	Publisher	Series No.
Ephrikian	G. Ricordi & Co.	PR 295

RECORDINGS

Label	Series No.
Angel	36004;S-36004
Epic	BC-1021
Epic	LC-3486

D MAJOR

Fanna I	Ricordi (Tomo)	Pincherle	Rinaldi
18	68	200	Op. 36, No. 4

PUBLICATIONS

Violin & Orchestra

Editor	Publisher	Series No.
Malipiero	G. Ricordi & Co.	PR 355

D MAJOR

Fanna I	Ricordi (Tomo)	Pincherle	Rinaldi
19	69	201	Op. 36, No. 6

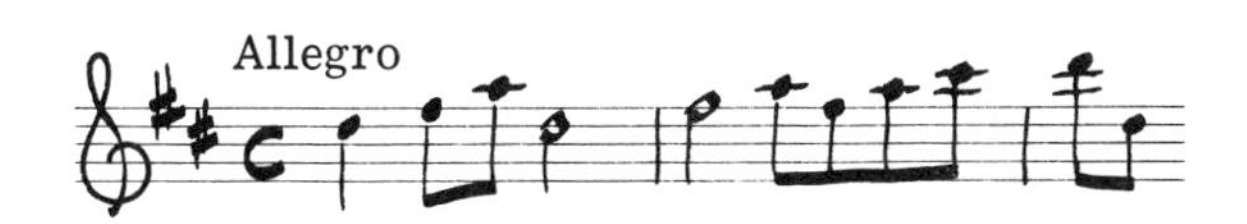

PUBLICATIONS

Violin & Orchestra

Editor	Publisher	Series No.
Malipiero	G. Ricordi & Co.	PR 356

D MAJOR

Fanna I	Ricordi (Tomo)	Pincherle	Rinaldi
30	84	153	Op. 8, No. 11 (Op. 36, No. 12)

PUBLICATIONS

Violin & Orchestra

Editor	Publisher	Series No.
Malipiero	G. Ricordi & Co.	PR 446

RECORDINGS*

*See Appendix E

D MAJOR

Concerto for 2 Violins

Fanna I	Ricordi (Tomo)	Pincherle	Rinaldi
35	89	190	Op. 21, No. 8

PUBLICATIONS

Violin & Orchestra

Editor	Publisher	Series No.
Malipiero	G. Ricordi & Co.	PR 451

D MAJOR

Concerto for 2 Violins

Fanna I	Ricordi (Tomo)	Pincherle	Rinaldi
41	108	189	Op. 21, No. 7

PUBLICATIONS

Violin & Orchestra

Editor	Publishers	Series No.
Malipiero	G. Ricordi & Co.	PR 558

Violin & Piano

Editor	Publishers	Series No.
	International Music Co.	

RECORDINGS

Label	Series No.
Columbia	ML-5604; MS-6204
Nonesuch	9179
Nonesuch	71022

D MAJOR

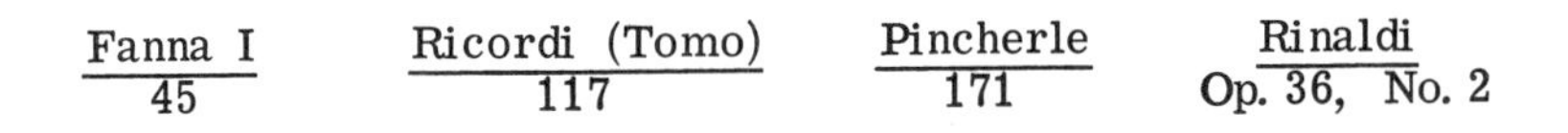

Fanna I	Ricordi (Tomo)	Pincherle	Rinaldi
45	117	171	Op. 36, No. 2

PUBLICATIONS

Violin & Orchestra

Editor	Publishers	Series No.
Malipiero	G. Ricordi & Co.	PR 567

Violin & Piano

Editor	Publishers	Series No.
Bellezza	G. Ricordi & Co.	129591

D MAJOR

"Per la S. S. Assunzione di Maria Vergine"

Fanna I	Ricordi (Tomo)	Pincherle	Rinaldi
62	141	164	Op. 54, No. 2

PUBLICATIONS

Violin & Orchestra

Editor	Publishers	Series No.
Malipiero	G. Ricordi & Co.	PR 591

Violin & Piano

Editor	Publishers	Series No.
Bellezza	G. Ricordi & Co.	129592

RECORDINGS

Label	Series No.
Seraphim	S-60118

D MAJOR

Fanna I	Ricordi (Tomo)	Pincherle	Rinaldi
80	174	186	Op. 33, No. 17

PUBLICATIONS

Violin & Orchestra

Editor	Publisher	Series No.
Malipiero	G. Ricordi & Co.	PR 699

D MAJOR

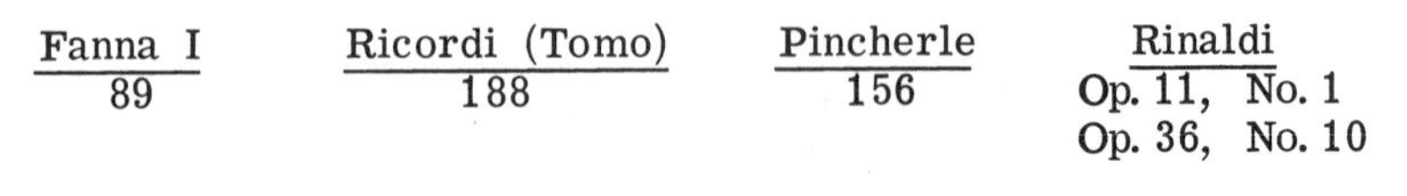

Fanna I	Ricordi (Tomo)	Pincherle	Rinaldi
89	188	156	Op. 11, No. 1 Op. 36, No. 10

PUBLICATIONS

Violin & Orchestra

Editor	Publishers	Series No.
Malipiero	G. Ricordi & Co.	PR 713

D MAJOR

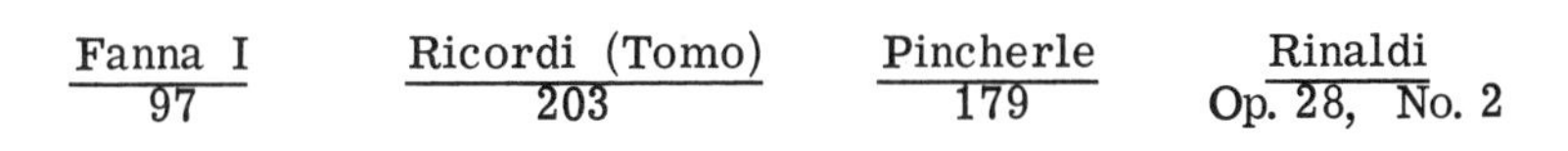

Fanna I	Ricordi (Tomo)	Pincherle	Rinaldi
97	203	179	Op. 28, No. 2

PUBLICATIONS

Violin & Orchestra

Editor	Publishers	Series No.
Malipiero	G. Ricordi & Co.	PR 753

D MAJOR

Fanna I	Ricordi (Tomo)	Pincherle	Rinaldi
116	261	182	Op. 31, No. 15

PUBLICATIONS

Violin & Orchestra

Editor	Publisher	Series No.
Malipiero	G. Ricordi & Co.	PR 886

Violin & Piano

Editor	Publisher	Series No.
Bellezza	G. Ricordi & Co.	129773

D MAJOR

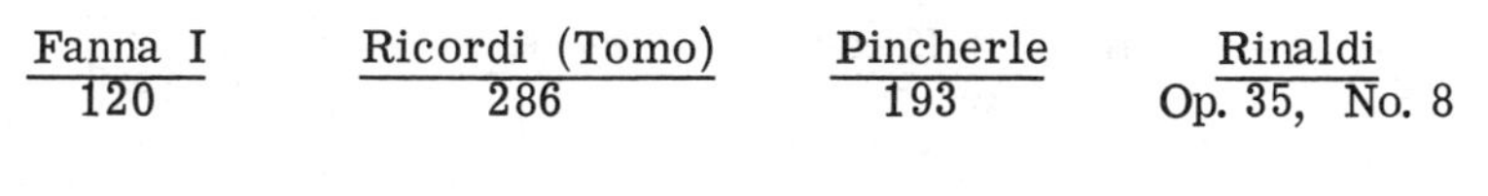

Fanna I	Ricordi (Tomo)	Pincherle	Rinaldi
120	286	193	Op. 35, No. 8

PUBLICATIONS

Violin & Orchestra

Editor	Publishers	Series No.
Malipiero	G. Ricordi & Co.	PR 936

D MAJOR

Fanna I	Ricordi (Tomo)	Pincherle	Rinaldi
124	294	192	Op. 35, No. 3

PUBLICATIONS

Violin & Orchestra

Editor	Publisher	Series No.
Malipiero	G. Ricordi & Co.	PR 944

D MAJOR

Fanna I	Ricordi (Tomo)	Pincherle	Rinaldi
129	302	170	Op. 35, No. 14 Op. 61, No. 17

PUBLICATIONS

Violin & Orchestra

Editor	Publisher	Series No.
Malipiero	G. Ricordi & Co.	PR 952

D MAJOR

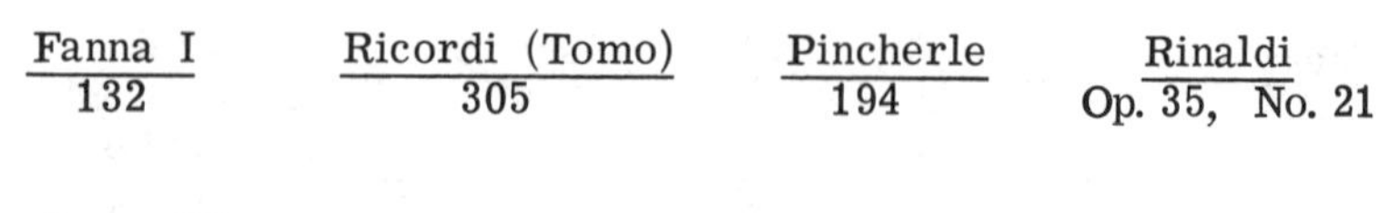

Fanna I	Ricordi (Tomo)	Pincherle	Rinaldi
132	305	194	Op. 35, No. 21

PUBLICATIONS

Violin & Orchestra

Editor	Publisher	Series No.
Malipiero	G. Ricordi & Co.	PR 955

D MAJOR

Fanna I	Ricordi (Tomo)	Pincherle	Rinaldi
133	306	195	Op. 35, No. 22

PUBLICATIONS

Violin & Orchestra

Editor	Publisher	Series No.
Malipiero	G. Ricordi & Co.	PR 956

RECORDINGS

Label	Series No.
Angel	36004; S-36004

D MAJOR

Fanna I	Ricordi (Tomo)	Pincherle	Rinaldi
134	307	196	Op. 35, No. 23

PUBLICATIONS

Violin & Orchestra

Editor	Publisher	Series No.
Malipiero	G. Ricordi & Co.	PR 957

D MAJOR

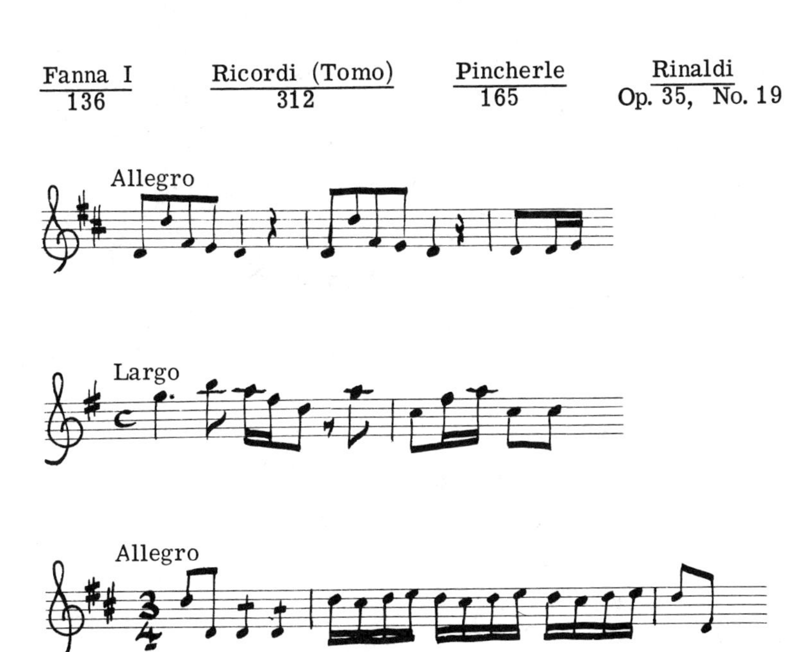

PUBLICATIONS

Violin & Orchestra

Editor	Publisher	Series No.
Malipiero	G. Ricordi & Co.	PR 962

D MAJOR

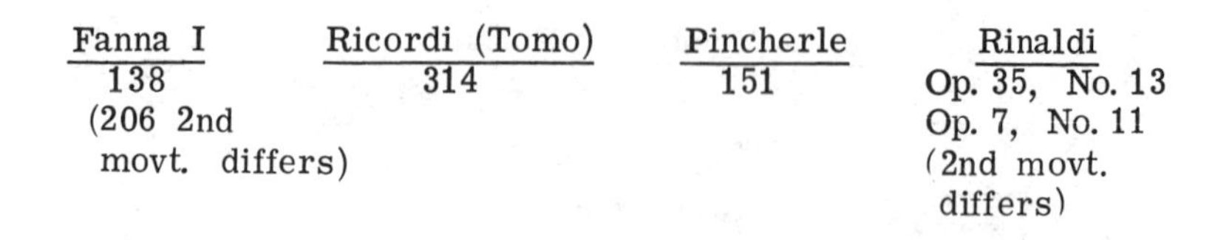

Fanna I	Ricordi (Tomo)	Pincherle	Rinaldi
138 (206 2nd movt. differs)	314	151	Op. 35, No. 13 Op. 7, No. 11 (2nd movt. differs)

PUBLICATIONS

Violin & Orchestra

Editor	Publisher	Series No.
Malipiero	G. Ricordi & Co.	PR 964

D MAJOR

Fanna I	Ricordi (Tomo)	Pincherle	Rinaldi
149	331	173	

PUBLICATIONS

Violin & Orchestra

Editor	Publisher	Series No.
Malipiero	G. Ricordi & Co.	PR 981

D MAJOR

Fanna I	Ricordi (Tomo)	Pincherle	Rinaldi
153	335	167	

PUBLICATIONS

Violin & Orchestra

Editor	Publisher	Series No.
Malipiero	G. Ricordi & Co.	PR 985

D MAJOR

Fanna I	Ricordi (Tomo)	Pincherle	Rinaldi
158	343	161	Op. 61, No. 4

PUBLICATIONS

Violin & Orchestra

Editor	Publisher	Series No.
Malipiero	G. Ricordi & Co.	PR 993

D MAJOR

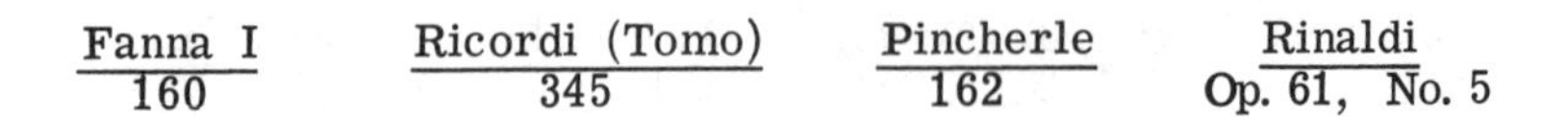

Fanna I	Ricordi (Tomo)	Pincherle	Rinaldi
160	345	162	Op. 61, No. 5

PUBLICATIONS

Violin & Orchestra

Editor	Publisher	Series No.
Malipiero	G. Ricordi & Co.	PR 995

D MAJOR

Fanna I	Ricordi (Tomo)	Pincherle	Rinaldi
162	347	163	Op. 61, No. 6

PUBLICATIONS

Violin & Orchestra

Editor	Publisher	Series No.
Malipiero	G. Ricordi & Co.	PR 997

RECORDINGS

Label	Series No.
Angel	36004;S-36004

D MAJOR

Fanna I	Ricordi (Tomo)	Pincherle	Rinaldi
178	414	147	Op. 3, No. 9

PUBLICATIONS

Violin & Orchestra

Editor	Publisher	Series No.
Malipiero	G. Ricordi & Co.	PR 1089
	Bärenreiter-Verlag	355

Violin & Piano

Editor	Publisher	Series No.
Dandelot	Editions Max Eschig (Assoc. Music Pub., U. S. agent)	

RECORDINGS*

Label	Series No.
Angel	35087
Angel	45030
Vox	STPL-513010 (movt. excerpt only)

*See Appendix E

D MAJOR

Fanna I	Ricordi (Tomo)	Pincherle	Rinaldi
190	428	149	Op. 4, No. 11

PUBLICATIONS

Violin & Orchestra

Editor	Publisher	Series No.
Ephrikian	G. Ricordi & Co.	PR 1103

RECORDINGS*

*See Appendix E

D MAJOR

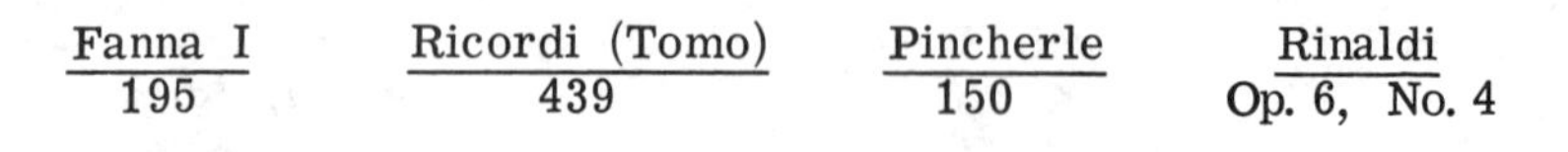

Fanna I	Ricordi (Tomo)	Pincherle	Rinaldi
195	439	150	Op. 6, No. 4

PUBLICATIONS

Violin & Orchestra

Editor	Publisher	Series No.
Malipiero	G. Ricordi & Co.	PR 1114

D MAJOR

Fanna I	Ricordi (Tomo)	Pincherle	Rinaldi
206 (138 2nd movt. differs)	452	151	Op. 7, No. 11 (Op. 35, No. 13) 2nd movt. differs

PUBLICATIONS

Violin & Orchestra

Editor	Publisher	Series No.
Malipiero	G. Ricordi & Co.	PR 1126
Schroeder	Eulenburg [pocket score] (C. F. Peters Corp. , U. S. agent)	

D MAJOR

Fanna I	Ricordi (Tomo)	Pincherle	Rinaldi
207	453	152	Op. 7, No. 12

PUBLICATIONS

Violin & Orchestra

Editor	Publisher	Series No.
Malipiero	G. Ricordi & Co.	PR 1128
Schroeder	Eulenburg [pocket score] (C. F. Peters Corp., U. S. agent)	

D MAJOR

Fanna I	Ricordi (Tomo)	Pincherle	Rinaldi
218	482	158	

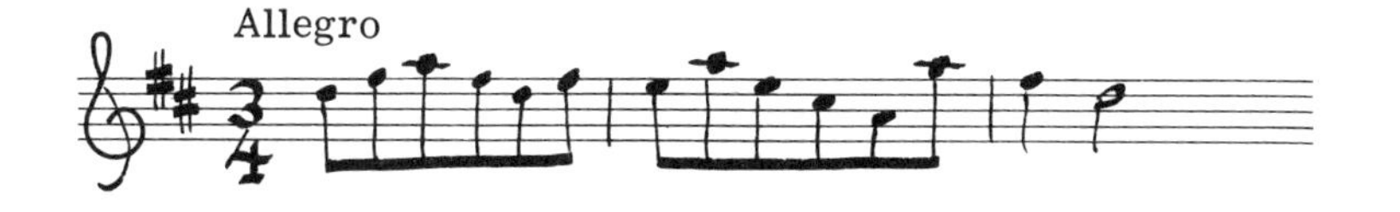

D MAJOR

Concerto for 2 Violins

Fanna I	Ricordi (Tomo)	Pincherle	Rinaldi
222	486	159	

D MAJOR

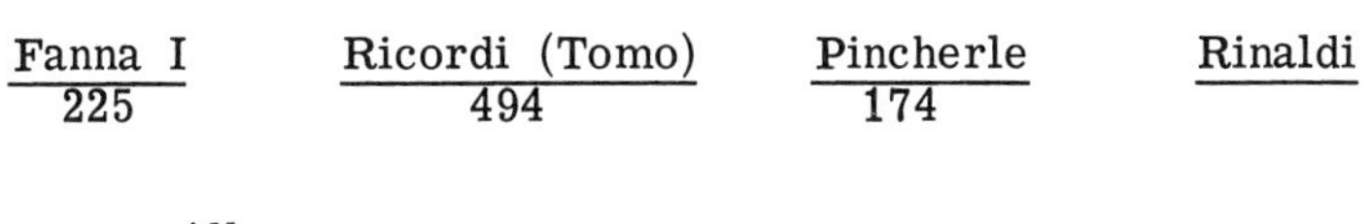

Fanna I	Ricordi (Tomo)	Pincherle	Rinaldi
225	494	174	

D MAJOR

Fanna I	Ricordi (Tomo)	Pincherle	Rinaldi
228	497	177	

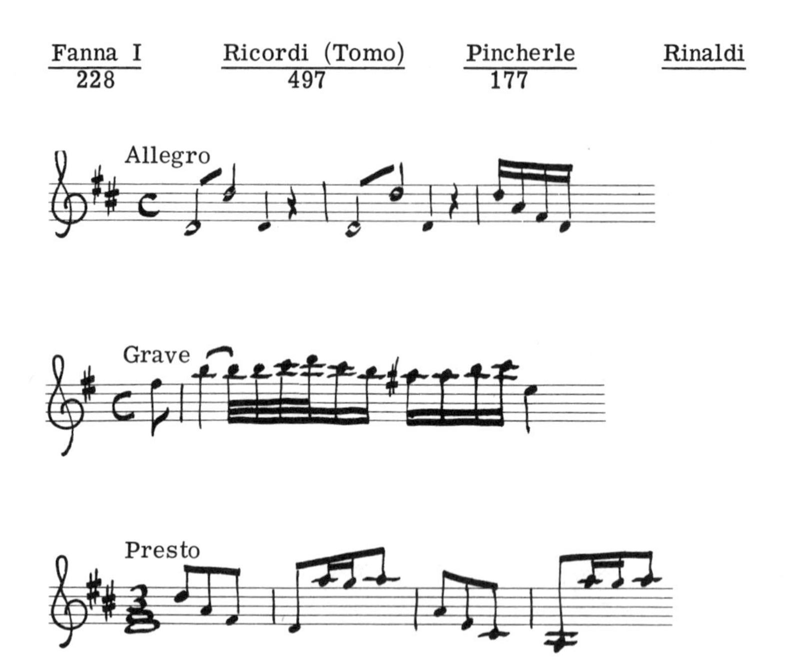

D MAJOR

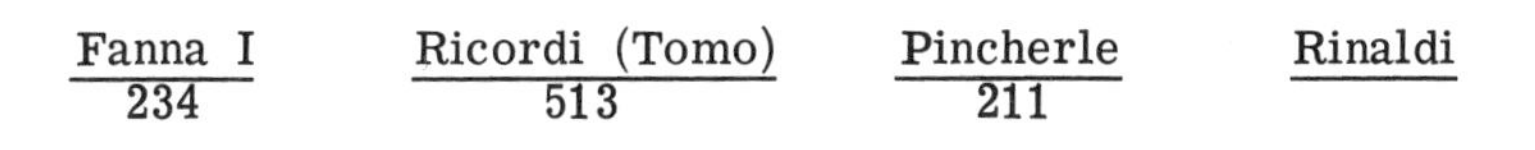

Fanna I	Ricordi (Tomo)	Pincherle	Rinaldi
234	513	211	

D MAJOR

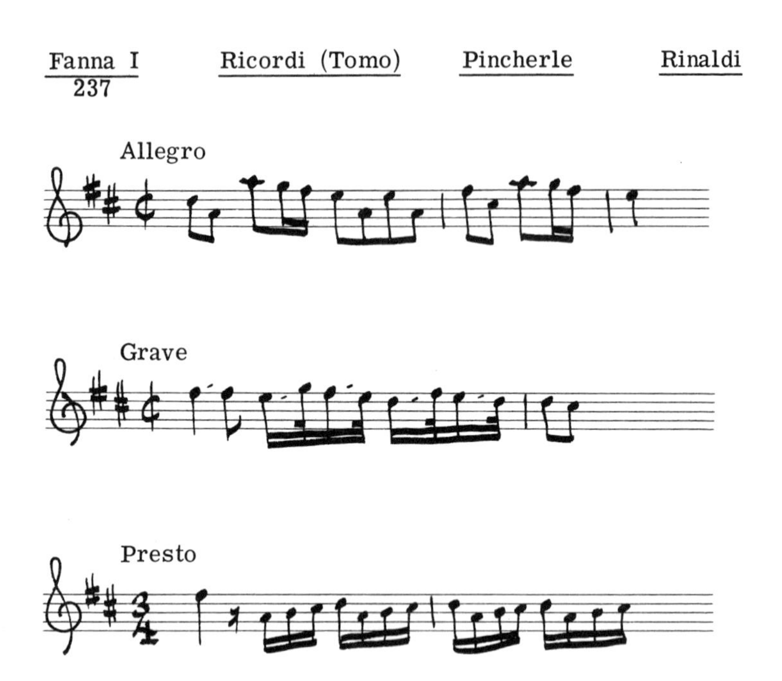
Fanna I
237
Ricordi (Tomo)
Pincherle
Rinaldi
Allegro
Grave
Presto

Begin: Concertos in D Minor

Scordatura

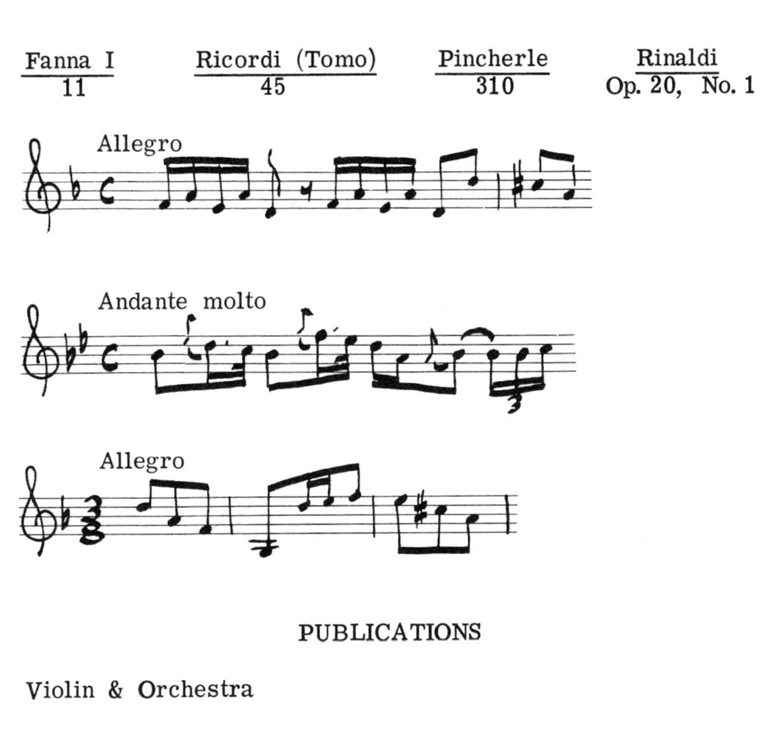

PUBLICATIONS

Violin & Orchestra

Editor	Publisher	Series No.
Malipiero	G. Ricordi & Co.	PR 310

RECORDINGS

Label	Series No.
Odyssey	32160053; 32160054

D MINOR

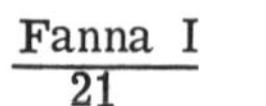

Fanna I	Ricordi (Tomo)	Pincherle	Rinaldi
21	74	316	Op. 36, No. 3

Allegro

Largo

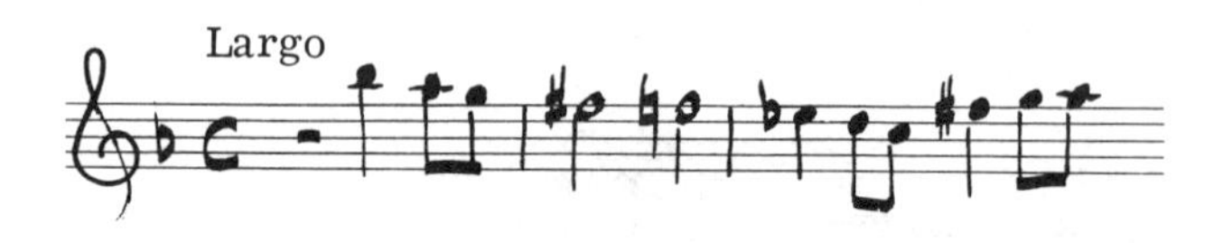

Presto

Allegro ma non molto

PUBLICATIONS

Violin & Orchestra

Editor	Publisher	Series No.
Malipiero	G. Ricordi & Co.	PR 361

D MINOR

per Pisendel

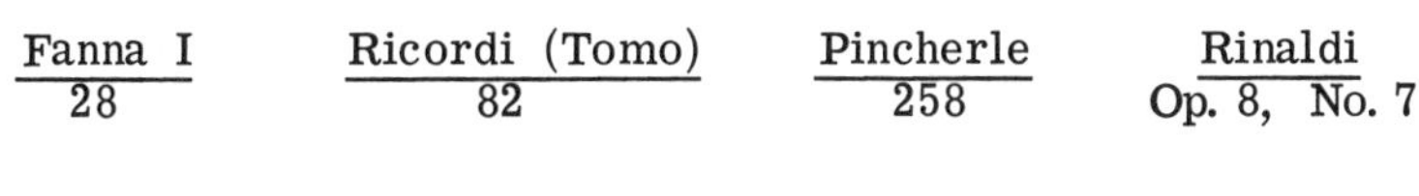

Fanna I	Ricordi (Tomo)	Pincherle	Rinaldi
28	82	258	Op. 8, No. 7

PUBLICATIONS

Violin & Orchestra

Editor	Publisher	Series No.
Malipiero	G. Ricordi & Co.	PR 444

Violin & Piano

Editor	Publisher	Series No.
Malipiero	G. Ricordi	129381

RECORDINGS*

Label	Series No.
Angel	S-36010

*See Appendix E

D MINOR

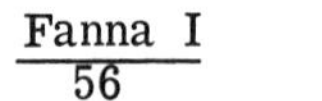

Fanna I	Ricordi (Tomo)	Pincherle	Rinaldi
56	131	260	Op. 9, No. 8

PUBLICATIONS

Violin & Orchestra

Editor	Publisher	Series No.
Malipiero	G. Ricordi & Co.	PR 581

RECORDINGS*

*See Appendix E

D MINOR

Concerto for 2 Violins

Fanna I	Ricordi (Tomo)	Pincherle	Rinaldi
100	209	281	Op. 27, No. 3

PUBLICATIONS

Violin & Orchestra

Editor	Publisher	Series No.
Malipiero	G. Ricordi & Co.	PR 759

Violin & Piano

Publisher
International Music Co.

RECORDINGS

Label	Series No.
Columbia	ML-5604; MS-6204

D MINOR

Fanna I	Ricordi (Tomo)	Pincherle	Rinaldi
113	258	293	Op. 31, No. 16

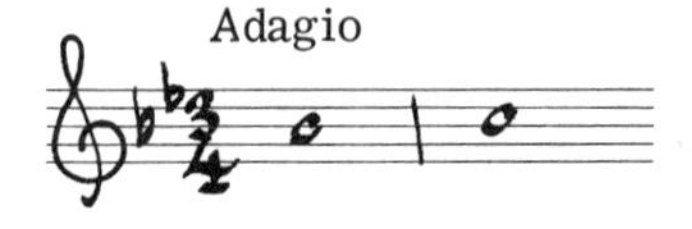

PUBLICATIONS

Violin & Orchestra

Editor	Publisher	Series No.
Malipiero	G. Ricordi & Co.	PR 883

D MINOR

Fanna I	Ricordi (Tomo)	Pincherle	Rinaldi
119	285	272	Op. 35, No. 4

Allegro

Largo

Allegro

PUBLICATIONS

Violin & Orchestra

Editor	Publisher	Series No.
Malipiero	G. Ricordi & Co.	PR 935

D MINOR

Fanna I	Ricordi (Tomo)	Pincherle	Rinaldi
126	296	312	Op. 35, No. 5

PUBLICATIONS

Violin & Orchestra

Editor	Publisher	Series No.
Malipiero	G. Ricordi & Co.	PR 946

D MINOR

Fanna I	Ricordi (Tomo)	Pincherle	Rinaldi
142	324	269	Op. 61, No. 3

PUBLICATIONS

Violin & Orchestra

Editor	Publisher	Series No.
Malipiero	G. Ricordi & Co.	PR 974

D MINOR

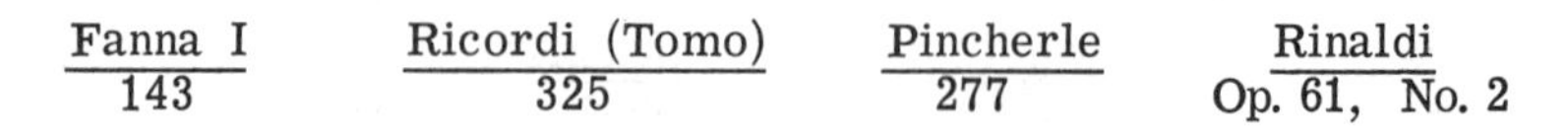

Fanna I	Ricordi (Tomo)	Pincherle	Rinaldi
143	325	277	Op. 61, No. 2

PUBLICATIONS

Violin & Orchestra

Editor	Publisher	Series No.
Malipiero	G. Ricordi & Co.	PR 975

D MINOR

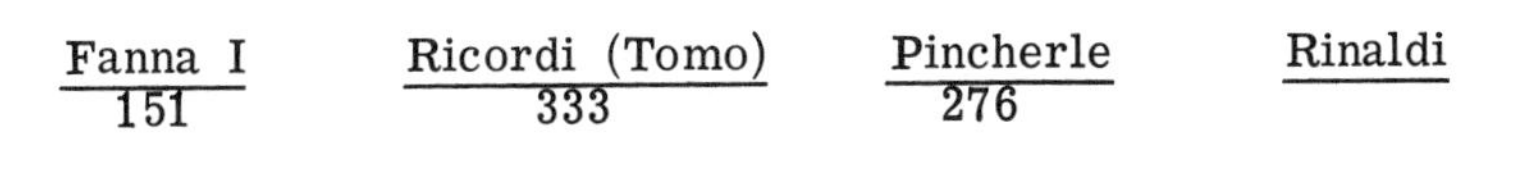

Fanna I	Ricordi (Tomo)	Pincherle	Rinaldi
151	333	276	

PUBLICATIONS

Violin & Orchestra

Editor	Publisher	Series No.
Malipiero	G. Ricordi & Co.	PR 983

D MINOR

Fanna I	Ricordi (Tomo)	Pincherle	Rinaldi
154	336	270	Op. 61, No. 9

PUBLICATIONS

Violin & Orchestra

Editor	Publisher	Series No.
Malipiero	G. Ricordi & Co.	PR 986

D MINOR

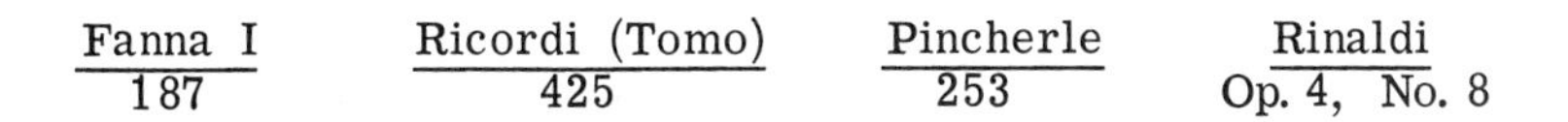

Fanna I	Ricordi (Tomo)	Pincherle	Rinaldi
187	425	253	Op. 4, No. 8

PUBLICATIONS

Violin & Orchestra

Editor	Publisher	Series No.
Ephrikian	G. Ricordi & Co.	PR 1100

RECORDINGS*

*See Appendix E

D MINOR

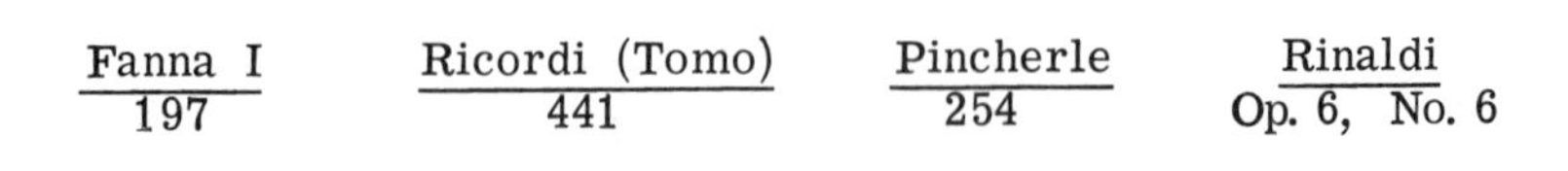

Fanna I	Ricordi (Tomo)	Pincherle	Rinaldi
197	441	254	Op. 6, No. 6

PUBLICATIONS

Violin & Orchestra

Editor	Publisher	Series No.
Malipiero	G. Ricordi & Co.	PR 1116

D MINOR

Fanna I	Ricordi (Tomo)	Pincherle	Rinaldi
212	463	263	Op. 12, No. 2

Allegro

Larghetto

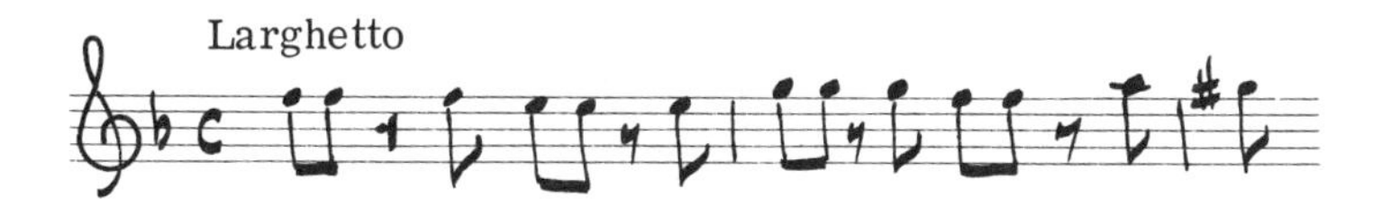

Allegro

PUBLICATIONS

Violin & Orchestra

Editor	Publisher	Series No.
Ephrikian	G. Ricordi & Co.	PR 1138

Begin: Concertos in E♭ Major

Fanna I	Ricordi (Tomo)	Pincherle	Rinaldi
9	38	429	Op. 33, No. 1

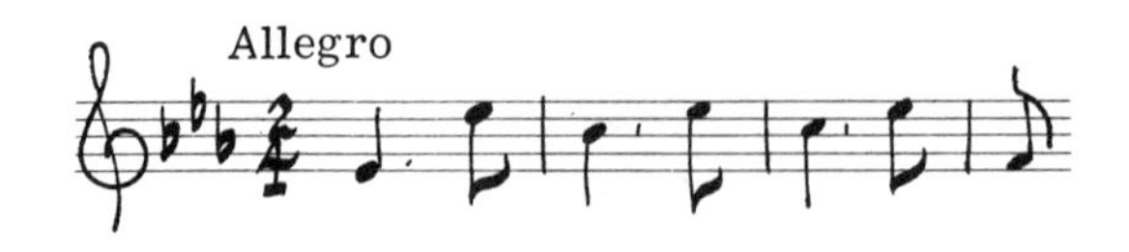

PUBLICATIONS

Violin & Orchestra

Editor	Publisher	Series No.
Ephrikian	G. Ricordi & Co.	PR 296

E♭ MAJOR

"La Tempesta Di Mere"

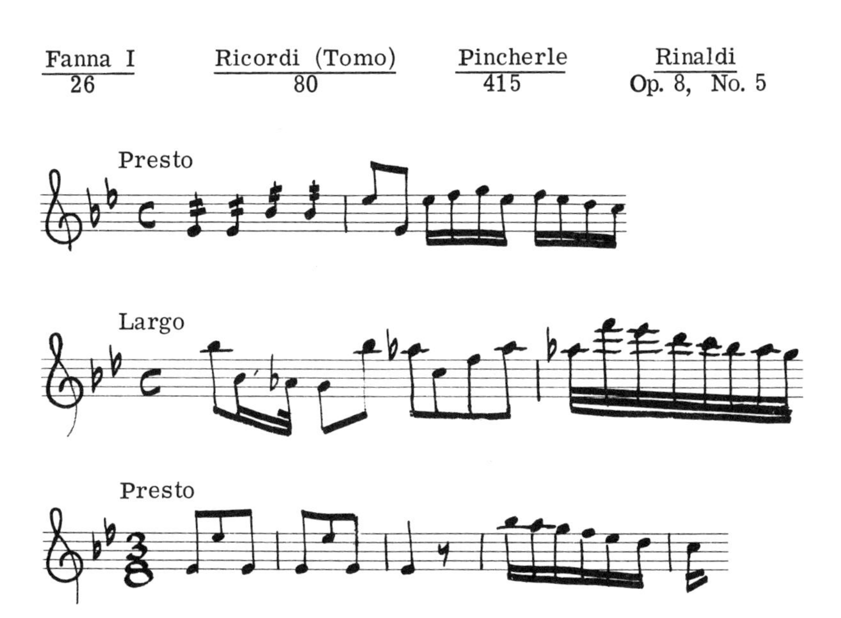

PUBLICATIONS

Violin & Orchestra

Editor	Publisher	Series No.
Malipiero	G. Ricordi & Co.	PR 442

RECORDINGS*

Label	Series No.
Epic	LC 3343
Mercury	50401-90401
Odeon	QALP-10013

*See Appendix E

E♭ MAJOR

Fanna I	Ricordi (Tomo)	Pincherle	Rinaldi
75	169	430	Op. 33, No. 16

PUBLICATIONS

Violin & Orchestra

Editor	Publisher	Series No.
Malipiero	G. Ricordi & Co.	PR 694

E♭ MAJOR

Fanna I	Ricordi (Tomo)	Pincherle	Rinaldi
92	193	439	Op. 36, No. 20

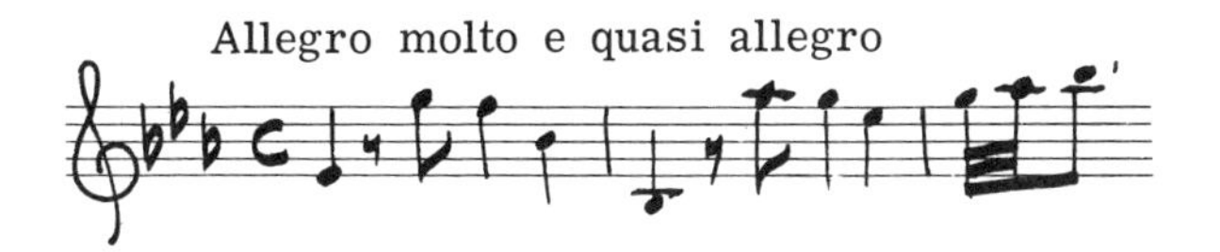

PUBLICATIONS

Violin & Orchestra

Editor	Publisher	Series No.
Malipiero	G. Ricordi & Co.	PR 718

E♭ MAJOR

Concerto for 2 Violins

Fanna I	Ricordi (Tomo)	Pincherle	Rinaldi
101	210	423	Op. 27, No. 4

PUBLICATIONS

Violin & Orchestra

Editor	Publisher	Series No.
Malipiero	G. Ricordi & Co.	PR 760

E♭ MAJOR

Fanna I	Ricordi (Tomo)	Pincherle	Rinaldi
102	227	425	Op. 31, No. 6

PUBLICATIONS

Violin & Orchestra

Editor	Publisher	Series No.
Malipiero	G. Ricordi & Co.	PR 827

E♭ MAJOR

Fanna I	Ricordi (Tomo)	Pincherle	Rinaldi
109	254	428	Op. 31, No. 21

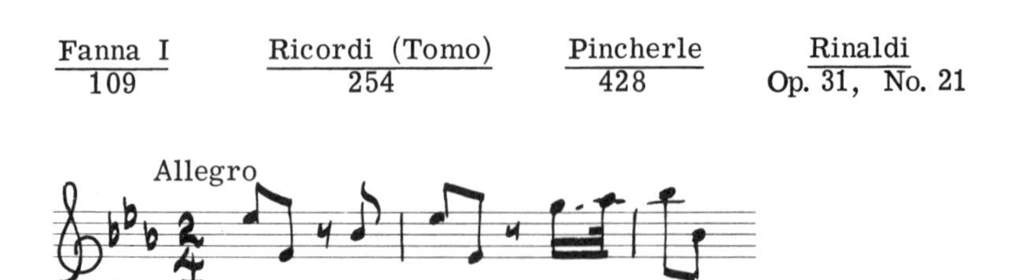

PUBLICATIONS

Violin & Orchestra

Editor	Publisher	Series No.
Malipiero	G. Ricordi & Co.	PR 879

E♭ MAJOR

Fanna I	Ricordi (Tomo)	Pincherle	Rinaldi
131	304	437	Op. 35, No. 18

PUBLICATIONS

Violin & Orchestra

Editor	Publisher	Series No.
Malipiero	G. Ricordi & Co.	PR 954

E♭ MAJOR

Fanna I	Ricordi (Tomo)	Pincherle	Rinaldi
156	340	420	Op. 61, No. 11

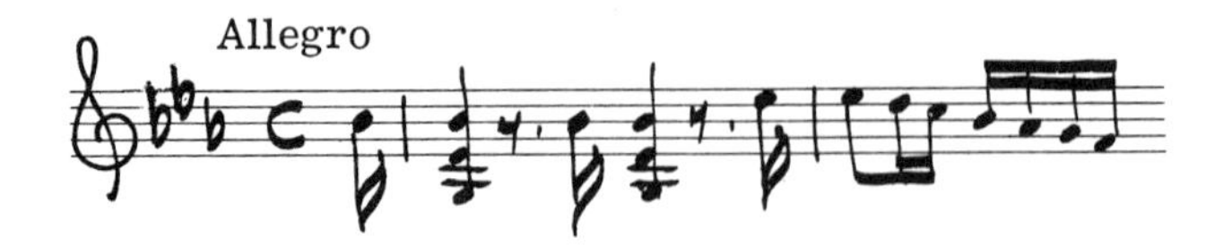

PUBLICATIONS

Violin & Orchestra

Editor	Publisher	Series No.
Malipiero	G. Ricordi & Co.	PR 990

E♭ MAJOR

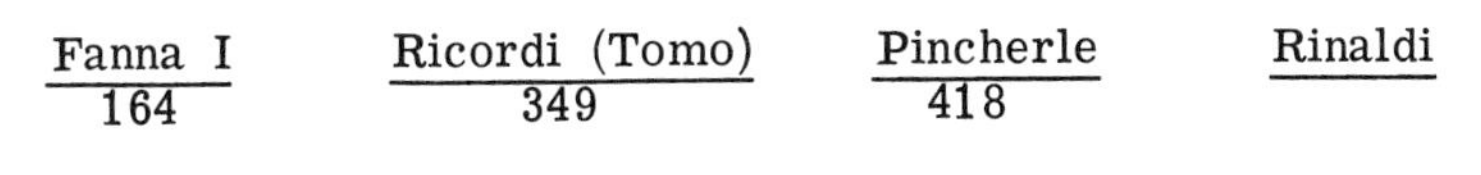

Fanna I	Ricordi (Tomo)	Pincherle	Rinaldi
164	349	418	

PUBLICATIONS

Violin & Orchestra

Editor	Publisher	Series No.
Malipiero	G. Ricordi & Co.	PR 999

E♭ MAJOR

Fanna I	Ricordi (Tomo)	Pincherle	Rinaldi
166	352	421	Op. 61, No. 14

PUBLICATIONS

Violin & Orchestra

Editor	Publisher	Series No.
Malipiero	G. Ricordi & Co.	PR 1002

E♭ MAJOR

Fanna I	Ricordi (Tomo)	Pincherle	Rinaldi
193	437	414 355	Op. 6, No. 2

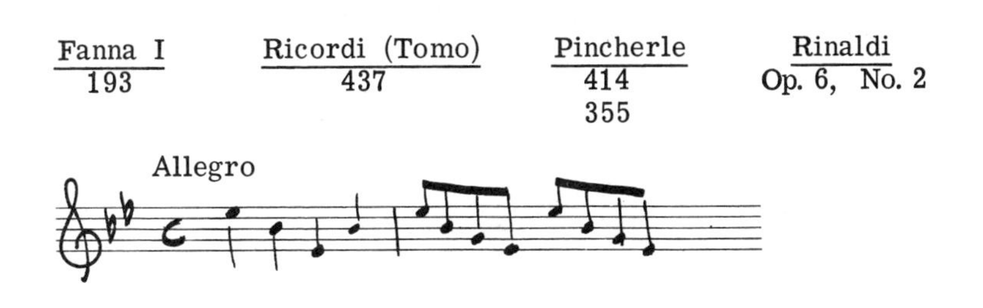

PUBLICATIONS

Violin & Orchestra

Editor	Publisher	Series No.
Malipiero	G. Ricordi & Co.	PR 1112

E♭ MAJOR

"Il Ritiro"

Fanna I	Ricordi (Tomo)	Pincherle	Rinaldi
231	502		

PUBLICATIONS

Violin & Orchestra

Editor	Publisher
Ephrikian	Kultura [for rent] (Boosey & Hawkes, Inc., U. S. agent)

Violin & Piano

Editor	Publisher
Ephrikian	Kultura (Boosey & Hawkes, Inc., U. S. agent)

Begin: Concertos in E Major

"Il Riposo"

Fanna I	Ricordi (Tomo)	Pincherle	Rinaldi
4	15	248	Op. 51, No. 2

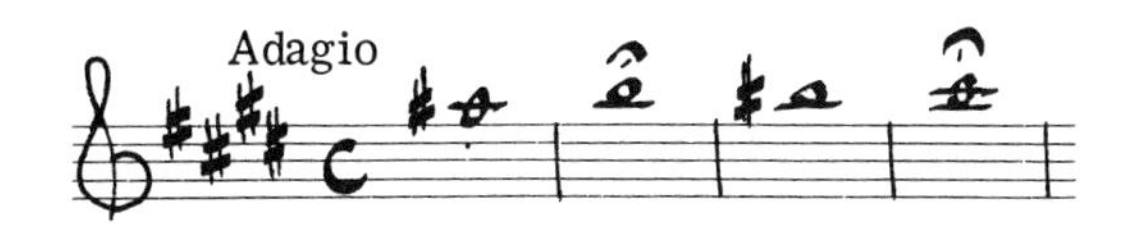

PUBLICATIONS

Violin & Orchestra

Editor	Publisher	Series No.
Fanna	G. Ricordi & Co.	PR 260

RECORDINGS

Label	Series No.
Epic	BC-102
Epic	LC-3486
Period	514
RCA Victor	LM-1880

E MAJOR

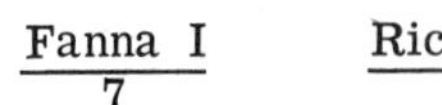

Fanna I	Ricordi (Tomo)	Pincherle	Rinaldi
7	29	244	Op. 33, No. 14

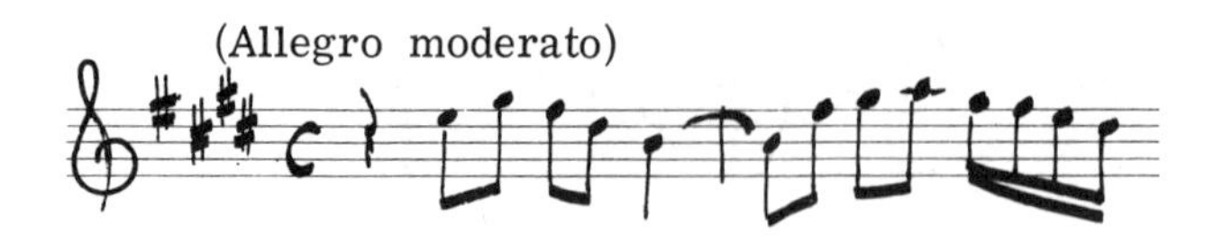

PUBLICATIONS

Violin & Orchestra

Editor	Publisher	Series No.
Ephrikian	G. Ricordi & Co.	PR 278

Violin & Piano

Editor	Publisher	Series No.
Ephrikian	G. Ricordi & Co.	129298

E MAJOR

"La Primavera"

Fanna I	Ricordi (Tomo)	Pincherle	Rinaldi
22	76	241	Op. 8, No. 1

PUBLICATIONS

Violin & Orchestra

Editor	Publisher	Series No.
Malipiero	G. Ricordi & Co.	PR 434
	Alexander Broude	
	Carisch	
	Edwin F. Kalmus [for sale or rent]	
	Hinrichsen Edition [for rent] (C. F. Peters Corp. U. S. agent)	
	Transatlantiques [for rent] (Theodore Presser Co., U. S. agent)	
	Eulenburg [pocket score]	

Violin & Piano

Editor	Publisher	Series No.
Soresina	G. Ricordi & Co.	128888
Sulyok-Tatriar	B. Schotts Söhne (Assoc. Music Pub., U. S. agent)	5911
	Hinrichsen Edition	H 2007

RECORDINGS*

*See Appendix E

E MAJOR

Fanna I	Ricordi (Tomo)	Pincherle	Rinaldi
48	123	242	Op. 9, No. 4 (Op. 31, No. 17 last movt. different)

PUBLICATIONS

Violin & Orchestra

Editor	Publisher	Series No.
Malipiero	G. Ricordi & Co.	PR 573

RECORDINGS*

*See Appendix E

E MAJOR

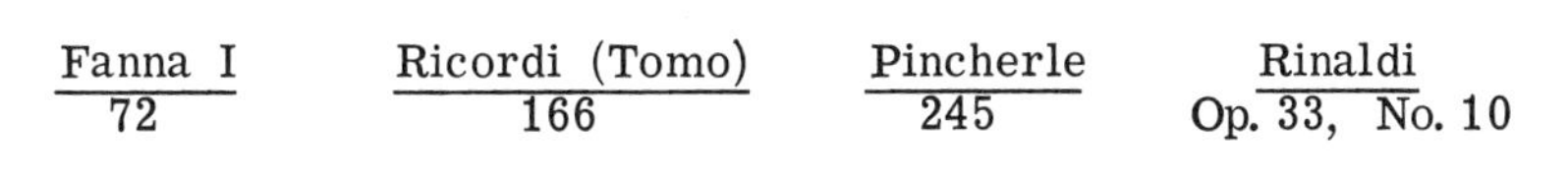

Fanna I	Ricordi (Tomo)	Pincherle	Rinaldi
72	166	245	Op. 33, No. 10

PUBLICATIONS

Violin & Orchestra

Editor	Publisher	Series No.
Malipiero	G. Ricordi & Co.	PR 691

E MAJOR

Fanna I	Ricordi (Tomo)	Pincherle	Rinaldi
84	180	247	Op. 36, No. 13

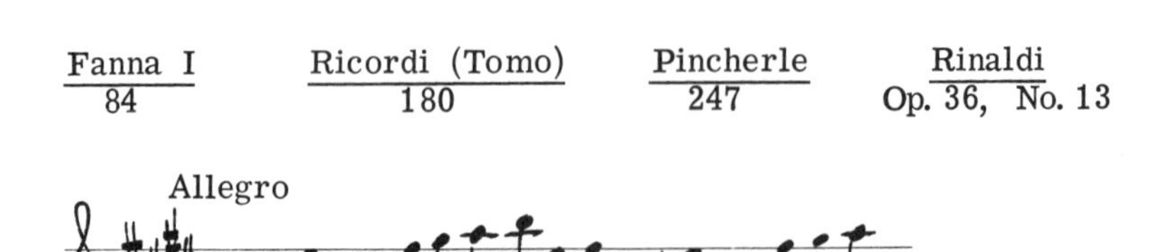

PUBLICATIONS

Violin & Orchestra

Editor	Publisher	Series No.
Malipiero	G. Ricordi & Co.	PR 705

E MAJOR

"L'Amoroso"

Fanna I	Ricordi (Tomo)	Pincherle	Rinaldi
127	297	246	Op. 35, No. 6

PUBLICATIONS

Violin & Orchestra

Editor	Publisher	Series No.
Malipiero	G. Ricordi & Co.	PR 947

RECORDINGS

Label	Series No.
Epic	BC-1021
Epic	LC-3486
Vox	STPL-513010 (movt. excerpts only)

E MAJOR

Fanna I	Ricordi (Tomo)	Pincherle	Rinaldi
145	327	243	

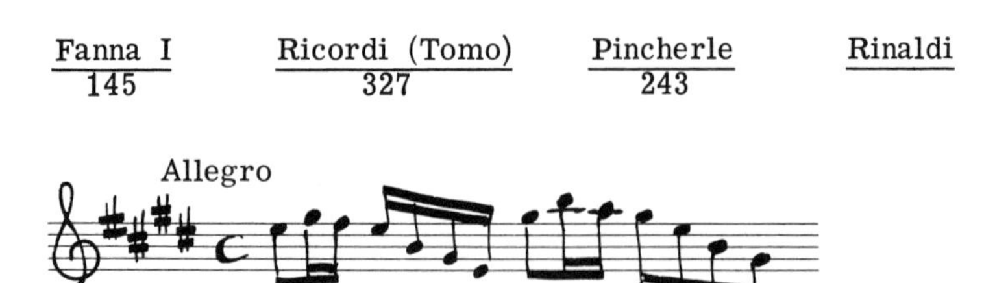

PUBLICATIONS

Violin & Orchestra

Editor	Publisher	Series No.
Malipiero	G. Ricordi & Co.	PR 977

E MAJOR

Fanna I	Ricordi (Tomo)	Pincherle	Rinaldi
179	417	240	Op. 3, No. 12

PUBLICATIONS

Violin & Orchestra

Editor	Publisher	Series No.
Malipiero	G. Ricordi & Co.	PR 1092
	Eulenburg [pocket score] (C. F. Peters Corp., U. S. agent)	

Violin & Piano

Editor	Publisher	Series No.
Borrel	Senart (Franco Colombo, U. S. agent)	5319
Kuechler	C. F. Peters Corp.	4379

RECORDINGS*

Label	Series No.
Bärenreiter	1832-2832

*See Appendix E

Begin: Concertos in E Minor

Fanna I	Ricordi (Tomo)	Pincherle	Rinaldi
37	93	144	Op. 56, No. 4

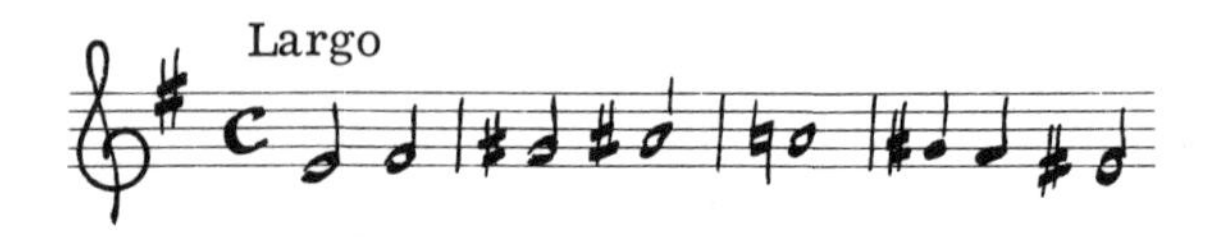

PUBLICATIONS

Violin & Orchestra

Editor	Publisher	Series No.
Malipiero	G. Ricordi & Co.	PR 455

E MINOR

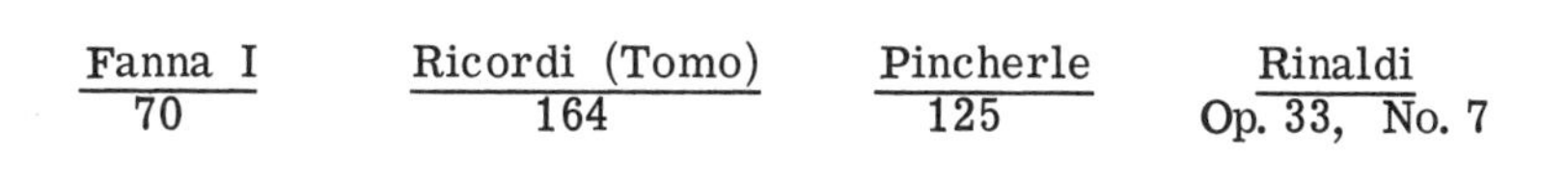

Fanna I	Ricordi (Tomo)	Pincherle	Rinaldi
70	164	125	Op. 33, No. 7

PUBLICATIONS

Violin & Orchestra

Editor	Publisher	Series No.
Malipiero	G. Ricordi & Co.	PR 689

E MINOR

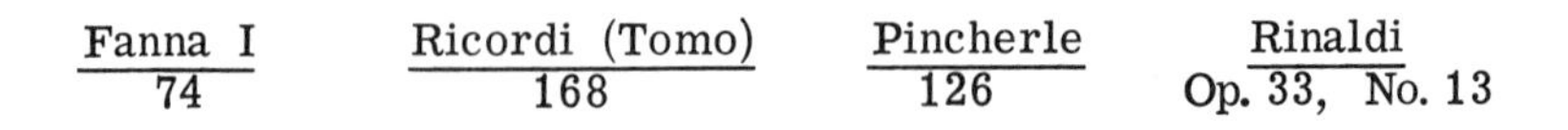

Fanna I	Ricordi (Tomo)	Pincherle	Rinaldi
74	168	126	Op. 33, No. 13

PUBLICATIONS

Violin & Orchestra

Editor	Publisher	Series No.
Malipiero	G. Ricordi & Co.	PR 693

E MINOR

Concerto for 4 Violins

Fanna I	Ricordi (Tomo)	Pincherle	Rinaldi
174	409	97	Op. 3, No. 4

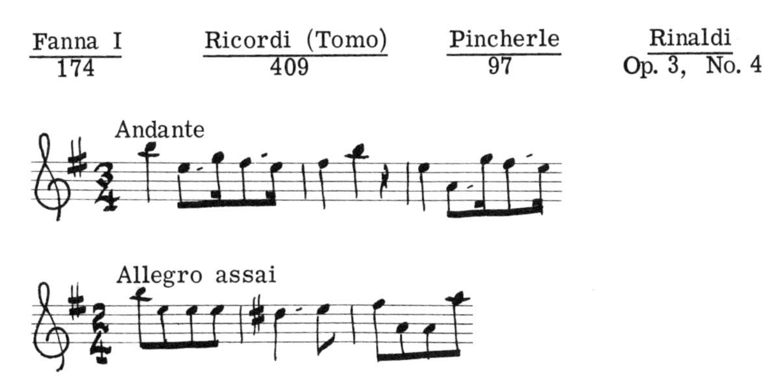

PUBLICATIONS

Violin & Orchestra

Editor	Publisher	Series No.
Malipiero	G. Ricordi & Co.	PR 1084

RECORDINGS*

*See Appendix E

E MINOR

Fanna I	Ricordi (Tomo)	Pincherle	Rinaldi
181	419	98	Op. 4, No. 2

PUBLICATIONS

Violin & Orchestra

Editor	Publisher	Series No.
Ephrikian	G. Ricordi & Co.	PR 1094
	Edwin F. Kalmus	[for sale or rent]
	Bärenreiter-Verlag	357

Violin & Piano

Editor	Publisher	Series No.
Upmeyer & Füssl	Bärenreiter-Verlag	3714

RECORDINGS*

*See Appendix E

E MINOR

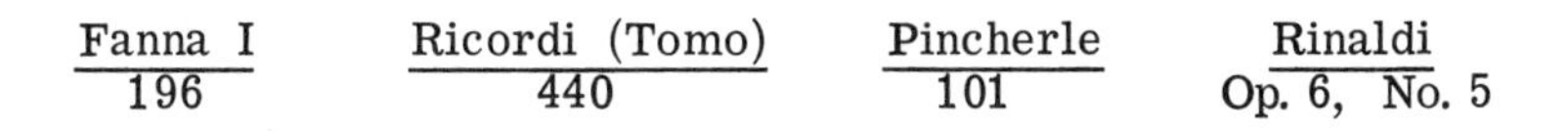

Fanna I	Ricordi (Tomo)	Pincherle	Rinaldi
196	440	101	Op. 6, No. 5

PUBLICATIONS

Violin & Orchestra

Editor	Publisher	Series No.
Malipiero	G. Ricordi & Co.	PR 1115

E MINOR

"Il Favorito"

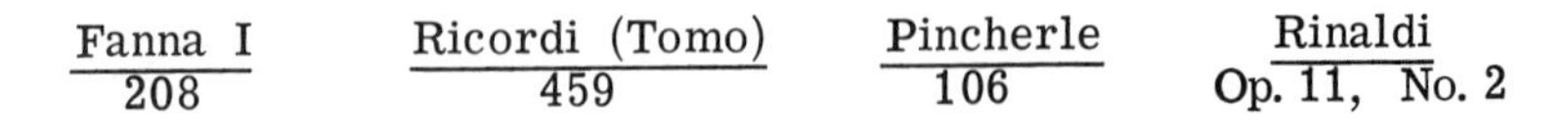

Fanna I	Ricordi (Tomo)	Pincherle	Rinaldi
208	459	106	Op. 11, No. 2

PUBLICATIONS

Violin & Orchestra

Editor	Publisher	Series No.
Malipiero	G. Ricordi & Co.	PR 1134

RECORDINGS

Label	Series No.
Epic	BC 1021
Epic	LC 3486
Phillips	500052; S900052

E MINOR

Fanna I	Ricordi (Tomo)	Pincherle	Rinaldi
216	480	108	

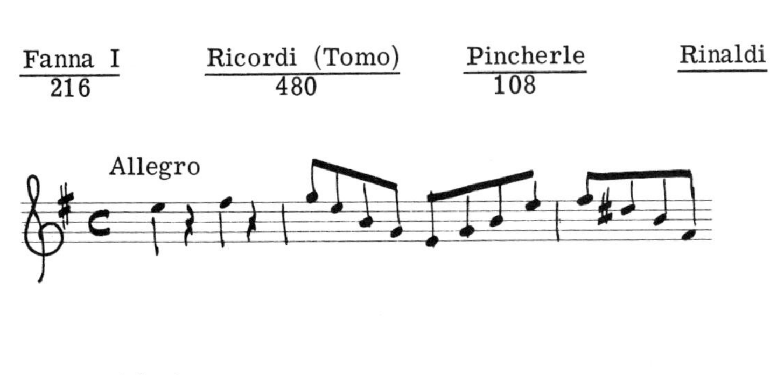

E MINOR

Fanna I	Ricordi (Tomo)	Pincherle	Rinaldi
220	484	109	Op. 16, No. 2

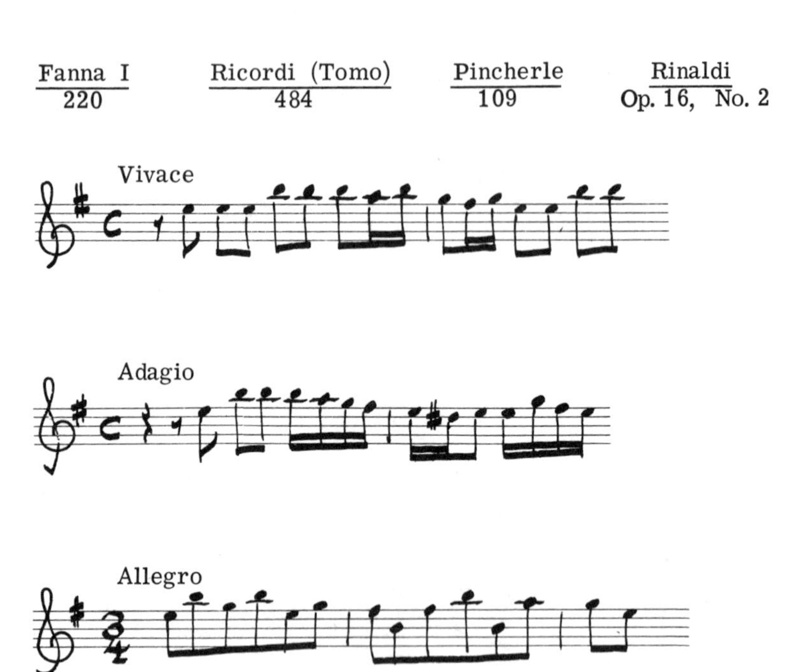

E MINOR

Fanna I	Ricordi (Tomo)	Pincherle	Rinaldi
238			

Allegro

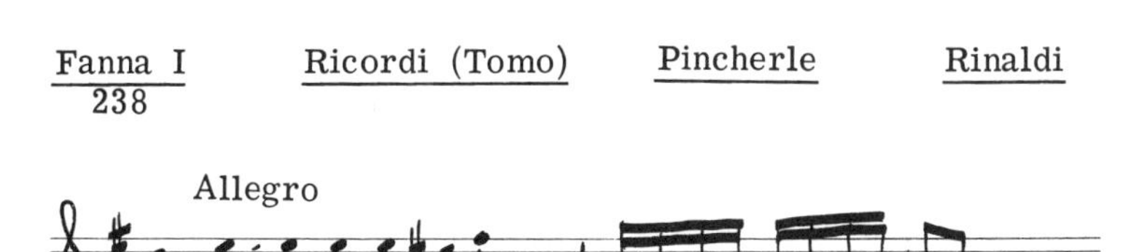

Adagio

Allegro

Begin: Concertos in F Major

Fanna I	Ricordi (Tomo)	Pincherle	Rinaldi
17	66	324	Op. 56, No. 1

Allegro ma poco

PUBLICATIONS

Violin & Orchestra

Editor	Publisher	Series No.
Malipiero	G. Ricordi & Co.	PR 353

F MAJOR

"Per la Solennita di San Lorenzo"

Fanna I	Ricordi (Tomo)	Pincherle	Rinaldi
20	70	290	Op. 31, No. 2

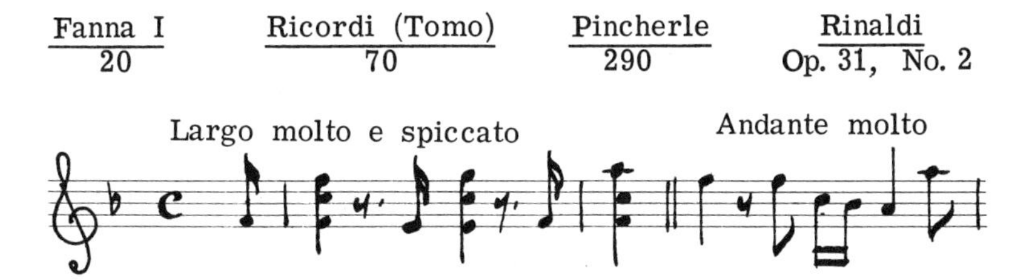

PUBLICATIONS

Violin & Orchestra

Editor	Publisher	Series No.
Malipiero	G. Ricordi & Co.	PR 357

RECORDINGS

Label	Series No.
Columbia	RL-6632
Listening, Inc.	6601

F MAJOR

"L'Autunno"

Fanna I	Ricordi (Tomo)	Pincherle	Rinaldi
24	78	257	Op. 8, No. 3

Allegro

Adagio molto

Allegro

PUBLICATIONS

Violin & Orchestra

Editor	Publisher	Series No.
Malipiero	G. Ricordi & Co.	PR 436
	Alexander Broude	
	Carisch	
	Edwin F. Kalmus [for sale or rent]	
	Hinrichsen Edition [for rent] (C. F. Peters Corp, U. S. agent)	
	Transatlantiques [for rent] (Theodore Presser Co., U. S. agent)	
	Eulenburg [pocket score] (C. F. Peters Corp., U. S. agent)	

Violin & Piano

Editor	Publisher	Series No.
Soresina	G. Ricordi & Co.	128890
Sulyok-Tatrar	B. Schotts Söhne (Assoc. Music Pub., U. S. agent)	5913
	Hinrichsen Edition	H-2009
	Transatlantiques	

RECORDINGS*

Label	Series No.
Angelicum	50036
Audio Fi	5938

*See Appendix E

F MAJOR

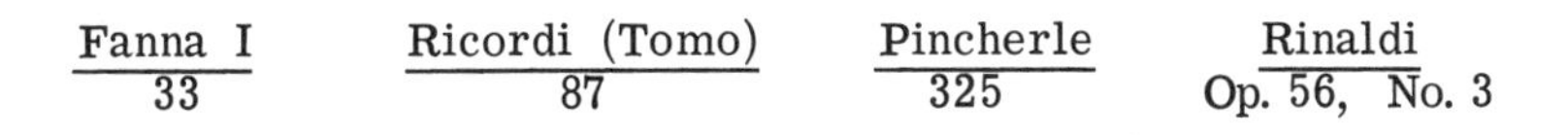

Fanna I	Ricordi (Tomo)	Pincherle	Rinaldi
33	87	325	Op. 56, No. 3

PUBLICATIONS

Violin & Orchestra

Editor	Publisher	Series No.
Malipiero	G. Ricordi & Co.	PR 449

F MAJOR

Concerto for 3 Violins

Fanna I	Ricordi (Tomo)	Pincherle	Rinaldi
34	88	278	Op. 23, No. 1 (Op. 61, No. 20)

PUBLICATIONS

Violin & Orchestra

Editor	Publisher	Series No.
Malipiero	G. Ricordi & Co.	PR 450

Violin & Piano

Editor	Publisher	Series No.
Bonelli	Zanibon (Franco Colombo, Inc., & C. F. Peters, U. S. agents)	3725
Medefind	International	

RECORDINGS

Label	Series No.
Angel	35088
Nonesuch	1022; 71022
Odyssey	32160053; 32160054
Phillips	500147; 900147

F MAJOR

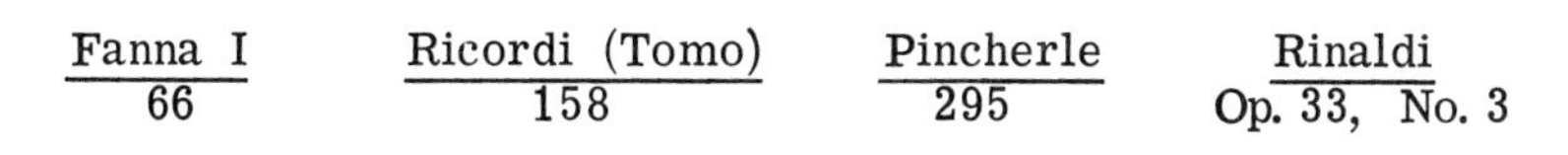

Fanna I	Ricordi (Tomo)	Pincherle	Rinaldi
66	158	295	Op. 33, No. 3

PUBLICATIONS

Violin & Orchestra

Editor	Publisher	Series No.
Malipiero	G. Ricordi & Co.	PR 683

F MAJOR

Fanna I	Ricordi (Tomo)	Pincherle	Rinaldi
71	165	296	Op. 33, No. 9

PUBLICATIONS

Violin & Orchestra

Editor	Publisher	Series No.
Malipiero	G. Ricordi & Co.	PR 690

F MAJOR

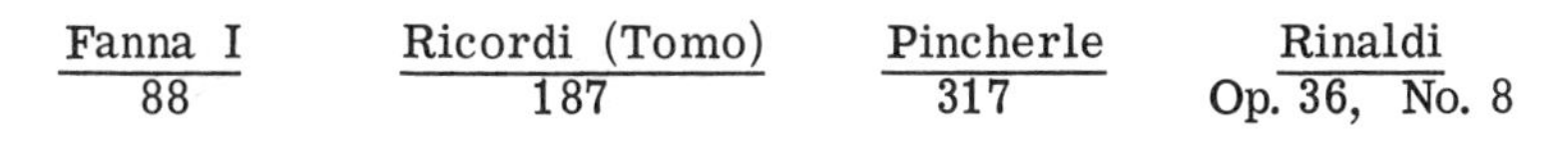

Fanna I	Ricordi (Tomo)	Pincherle	Rinaldi
88	187	317	Op. 36, No. 8

PUBLICATIONS

Violin & Orchestra

Editor	Publisher	Series No.
Malipiero	G. Ricordi & Co.	PR 712

F MAJOR

Fanna I	Ricordi (Tomo)	Pincherle	Rinaldi
128	301	314	Op. 35, No. 15

PUBLICATIONS

Violin & Orchestra

Editor	Publisher	Series No.
Malipiero	G. Ricordi & Co.	PR 951

F MAJOR

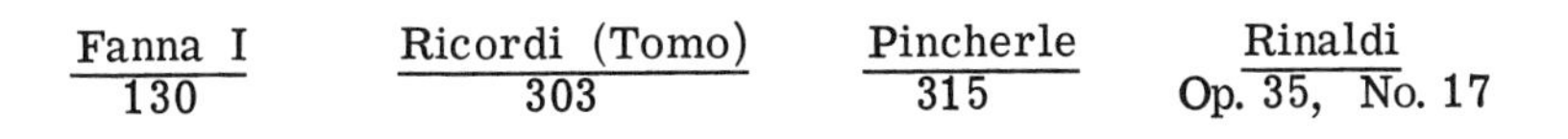

PUBLICATIONS

Violin & Orchestra

Editor	Publisher	Series No.
Malipiero	G. Ricordi & Co.	PR 953

F MAJOR

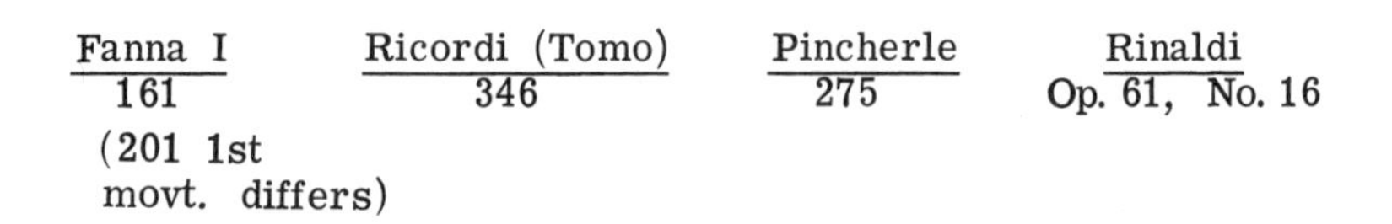

Fanna I	Ricordi (Tomo)	Pincherle	Rinaldi
161 (201 1st movt. differs)	346	275	Op. 61, No. 16

PUBLICATIONS

Violin & Orchestra

Editor	Publisher	Series No.
Malipiero	G. Ricordi & Co.	PR 996

F MAJOR

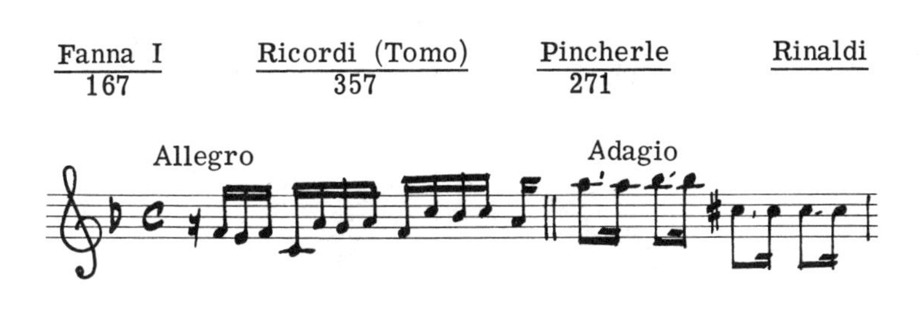

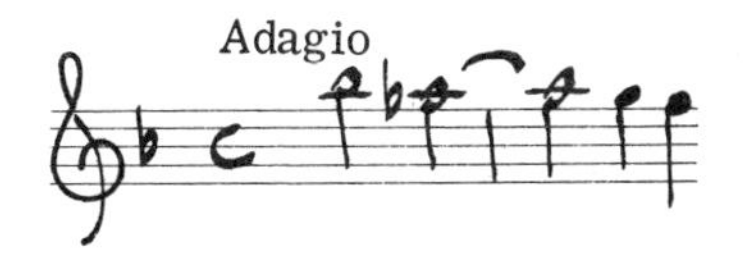

PUBLICATIONS

Violin & Orchestra

Editor	Publisher	Series No.
Malipiero	G. Ricordi & Co.	PR 1007

F MAJOR

Fanna I	Ricordi (Tomo)	Pincherle	Rinaldi
188	426	251	Op. 4, No. 9

PUBLICATIONS

Violin & Orchestra

Editor	Publisher	Series No.
Ephrikian	G. Ricordi & Co.	PR 1101

RECORDINGS*

*See Appendix E

F MAJOR

Fanna I	Ricordi (Tomo)	Pincherle	Rinaldi
201 (161 1st movt. differs)	446	255	Op. 7, No. 5

PUBLICATIONS

Violin & Orchestra

Editor	Publisher	Series No.
Malipiero	G. Ricordi & Co.	PR 1121

F MAJOR

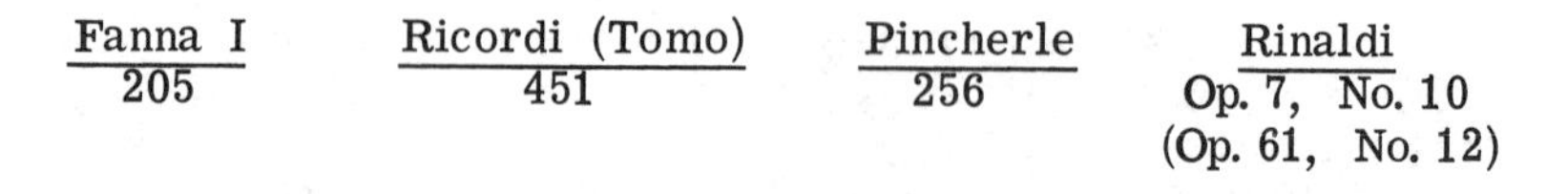

Fanna I	Ricordi (Tomo)	Pincherle	Rinaldi
205	451	256	Op. 7, No. 10 (Op. 61, No. 12)

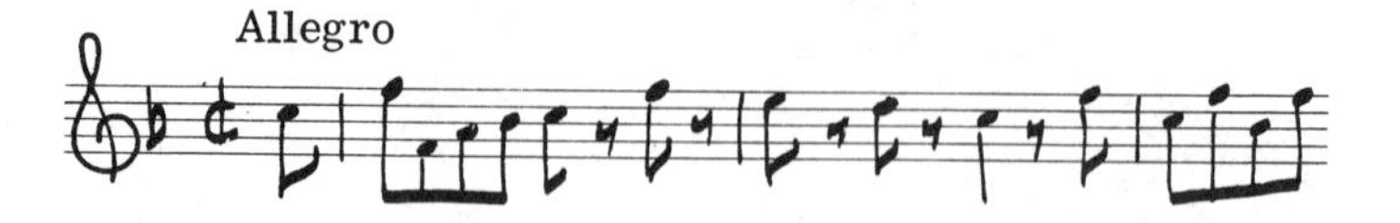

PUBLICATIONS

Violin & Orchestra

Editor	Publisher	Series No.
Malipiero	G. Ricordi & Co.	PR 1126

F MAJOR

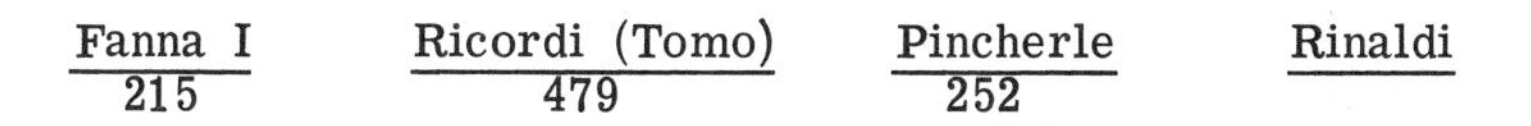

Fanna I	Ricordi (Tomo)	Pincherle	Rinaldi
215	479	252	

Begin: Concerto in F Minor

"L'Inverno"

Fanna I	Ricordi (Tomo)	Pincherle	Rinaldi
25	79	442	Op. 8, No. 4

PUBLICATIONS

Violin & Orchestra

Editor	Publishers	Series No.
Malipiero	G. Ricordi & Co.	PR 437
	Alexander Broude	
	Carisch	
	Edwin F. Kalmus [for sale or rent]	
	Hinrichsen Edition [for rent] (C. F. Peters Corp., U. S. agent)	
	Transatlantiques [for rent] (Theodore Presser Co., U. S. agent)	
	Eulenburg [pocket score]	

Violin & Piano

Editor	Publishers	Series No.
Soresina	G. Ricordi & Co.	128891
Sulyoh-Tatrar	B. Schotts Söhne (Assoc. Music Pub., U. S. agent)	5914
	Hinrichsen Edition	H 2010
	Transatlantiques	

RECORDINGS*

*See Appendix E

Begin: Concertos in G Major

Concerto for 2 Violins

Fanna I	Ricordi (Tomo)	Pincherle	Rinaldi
6	27	132	Op. 21, No. 1

PUBLICATIONS

Violin & Orchestra

Editor	Publisher	Series No.
Ephrikian	G. Ricordi & Co.	PR 276

RECORDINGS

Label	Series No.
Mercury	50425-90425

G MAJOR

Fanna I	Ricordi (Tomo)	Pincherle	Rinaldi
49	124	103	Op. 9, No. 10

Allegro

Largo cantabile

Allegro

PUBLICATIONS

Violin & Orchestra

Editor	Publisher	Series No.
Malipiero	G. Ricordi & Co.	PR 574
	C. F. Peters Corp. [for rent]	

RECORDINGS*

*See Appendix E

G MAJOR

Fanna I	Ricordi (Tomo)	Pincherle	Rinaldi
64	156	138	Op. 47, No. 1

PUBLICATIONS

Violin & Orchestra

Editor	Publisher	Series No.
Malipiero	G. Ricordi & Co.	PR 681

G MAJOR

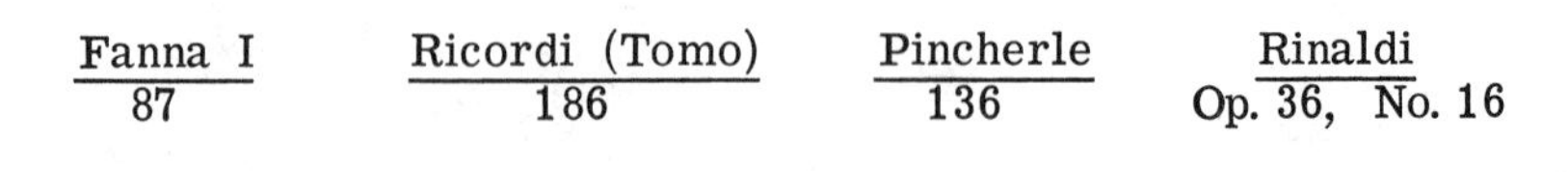

Fanna I	Ricordi (Tomo)	Pincherle	Rinaldi
87	186	136	Op. 36, No. 16

PUBLICATIONS

Violin & Orchestra

Editor	Publisher	Series No.
Malipiero	G. Ricordi & Co.	PR 711

G MAJOR

per Pisendel

Fanna I	Ricordi (Tomo)	Pincherle	Rinaldi
91	192	111	Op. 36, No. 17 (Op. 61, No. 7)

PUBLICATIONS

Violin & Orchestra

Editor	Publisher	Series No.
Malipiero	G. Ricordi & Co.	PR 717

G MAJOR

Fanna I	Ricordi (Tomo)	Pincherle	Rinaldi
96	202	117	Op. 28, No. 1

PUBLICATIONS

Violin & Orchestra

Editor	Publisher	Series No.
Malipiero	G. Ricordi & Co.	PR 752

RECORDINGS

Label	Series No.
Angelicum	5911
Harmonia - Mundi	30664

G MAJOR

Fanna I	Ricordi (Tomo)	Pincherle	Rinaldi
103	228	121	Op. 31, No. 4

PUBLICATIONS

Violin & Orchestra

Editor	Publisher	Series No.
Malipiero	G. Ricordi & Co.	PR 828

G MAJOR

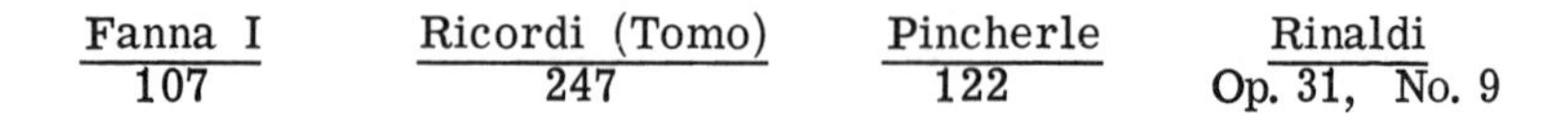

Fanna I	Ricordi (Tomo)	Pincherle	Rinaldi
107	247	122	Op. 31, No. 9

Allegro molto

Larghetto

Allegro

PUBLICATIONS

Violin & Orchestra

Editor	Publisher	Series No.
Malipiero	G. Ricordi & Co.	PR 847

G MAJOR

Fanna I	Ricordi (Tomo)	Pincherle	Rinaldi
110	255	124	Op. 31, No. 11

Allegro molto

Adagio

Allegro

PUBLICATIONS

Violin & Orchestra

Editor	Publisher	Series No.
Malipiero	G. Ricordi & Co.	PR 880

G MAJOR

Fanna I	Ricordi (Tomo)	Pincherle	Rinaldi
168	358	112	

PUBLICATIONS

Violin & Orchestra

Editor	Publisher	Series No.
Malipiero	G. Ricordi & Co.	PR 1008
	Bärenreiter-Verlag	3808

G MAJOR

Fanna I	Ricordi (Tomo)	Pincherle	Rinaldi
173	408	96	Op. 3, No. 3

PUBLICATIONS

Violin & Orchestra

Editor	Publisher	Series No.
Malipiero	G. Ricordi & Co.	PR 1083

RECORDINGS*

Label	Series No.
Bärenreiter	2822
Harmonia-Mundi	30664

*See Appendix E

G MAJOR

Fanna I	Ricordi (Tomo)	Pincherle	Rinaldi
182	420	99	Op. 4, No. 3

PUBLICATIONS

Violin & Orchestra

Editor	Publisher	Series No.
Ephrikian	G. Ricordi & Co.	PR 1095
	Bärenreiter-Verlag	
	Kalmus [for sale or rent]	

RECORDINGS*

*See Appendix E

G MAJOR

Fanna I	Ricordi (Tomo)	Pincherle	Rinaldi
191	429	100	Op. 4, No. 12

PUBLICATIONS

Violin & Orchestra

Editor	Publisher	Series No.
Ephrikian	G. Ricordi & Co.	PR 1104

RECORDINGS*

*See Appendix E

G MAJOR

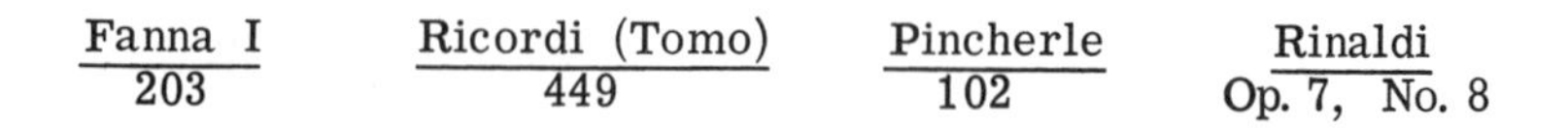

Fanna I	Ricordi (Tomo)	Pincherle	Rinaldi
203	449	102	Op. 7, No. 8

PUBLICATIONS

Violin & Orchestra

Editor	Publisher	Series No.
Malipiero	G. Ricordi & Co.	PR 1124

G MAJOR

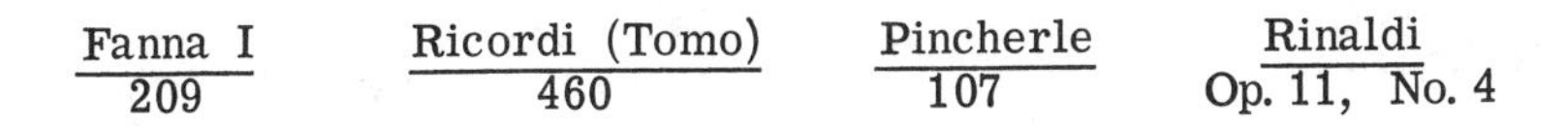

Fanna I	Ricordi (Tomo)	Pincherle	Rinaldi
209	460	107	Op. 11, No. 4

PUBLICATIONS

Violin & Orchestra

Editor	Publisher	Series No.
Malipiero	G. Ricordi & Co.	PR 1135

Begin: Concertos in G Minor

Fanna I	Ricordi (Tomo)	Pincherle	Rinaldi
16	65	337	Op. 8, No. 8 (Op. 36, No. 1)

PUBLICATIONS

Violin & Orchestra

Editor	Publisher	Series No.
Malipiero	G. Ricordi & Co.	PR 352

Violin & Piano

Editor	Publisher	Series No.
Malipiero	G. Ricordi & Co.	129380

G MINOR

"L'Estate"

Fanna I	Ricordi (Tomo)	Pincherle	Rinaldi
23	77	336	Op. 8, No. 2

PUBLICATIONS

Violin & Orchestra

Editor	Publishers	Series No.
Malipiero	G. Ricordi & Co.	PR 435
	Alexander Broude	
	Carisch	
	Kalmus [for sale or rent]	
	Transatlantiques [for rent]	
	Hinrichsen Edition [for rent]	
	Eulenburg [pocket score]	

Violin & Piano

Editor	Publishers	Series No.
Soresina	G. Ricordi & Co.	128889
Sulyok - Tatrar	B. Schotts Söhne	SCH-5912
	Transatlantiques	
	Hinrichsen Edition (C. F. Peters Corp., U. S. agent)	H-2008

G MINOR

"L'Estate (cont'd.)

RECORDINGS*

Label	Series No.
Columbia	MS-6204
Vox	STPL-53010 (movt. excerpt only)

*See Appendix E

G MINOR

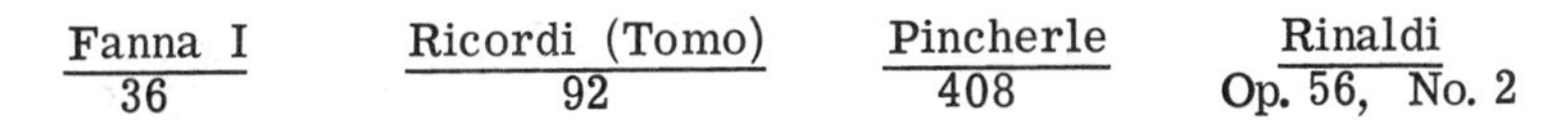

Fanna I	Ricordi (Tomo)	Pincherle	Rinaldi
36	92	408	Op. 56, No. 2

PUBLICATIONS

Violin & Orchestra

Editor	Publisher	Series No.
Malipiero	G. Ricordi & Co.	PR 454

G MINOR

Fanna I	Ricordi (Tomo)	Pincherle	Rinaldi
52	127	339	Op. 9, No. 3 Op. 11, No. 6

PUBLICATIONS

Violin & Orchestra

Editor	Publishers	Series No.
Malipiero	G. Ricordi & Co.	PR 577
Casella	Carisch	

Violin & Piano

Editor	Publishers
Orszagh-Nagy	Kultura (Boosey & Hawkes, Inc., U. S. agent)

RECORDINGS*

*See Appendix E

G MINOR

Fanna I	Ricordi (Tomo)	Pincherle	Rinaldi
81	175	379	Op. 33, No. 19

PUBLICATIONS

Violin & Orchestra

Editor	Publisher	Series No.
Malipiero	G. Ricordi & Co.	PR 700

G MINOR

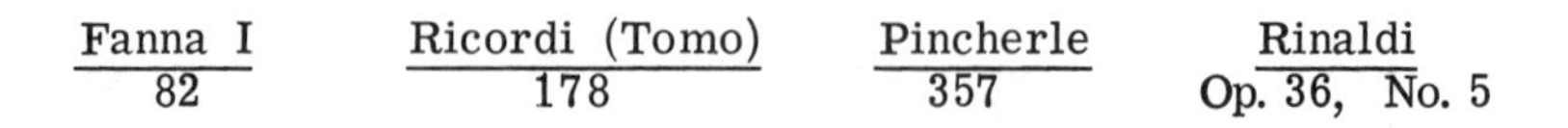

Fanna I	Ricordi (Tomo)	Pincherle	Rinaldi
82	178	357	Op. 36, No. 5

PUBLICATIONS

Violin & Orchestra

Editor	Publisher	Series No.
Malipiero	G. Ricordi & Co.	PR 703

G MINOR

Concerto for 2 Violins

Fanna I	Ricordi (Tomo)	Pincherle	Rinaldi
98	207	366	Op. 27, No. 2

PUBLICATIONS

Violin & Orchestra

Editor	Publisher	Series No.
Malipiero	G. Ricordi & Co.	PR 757

Violin & Piano

Publisher
International

RECORDINGS

Label	Series No.
Columbia	ML-5604; MS-6204

G MINOR

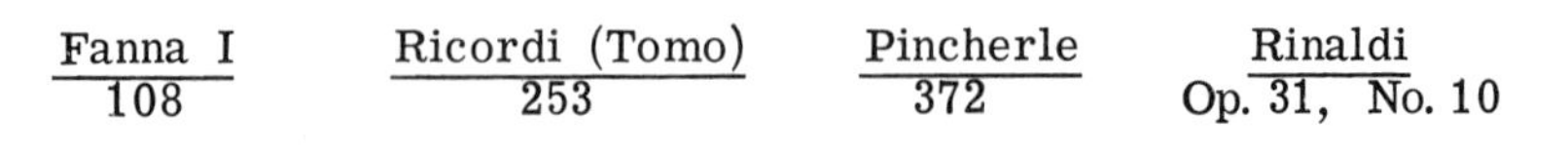

Fanna I	Ricordi (Tomo)	Pincherle	Rinaldi
108	253	372	Op. 31, No. 10

PUBLICATIONS

Violin & Orchestra

Editor	Publisher	Series No.
Malipiero	G. Ricordi & Co.	PR 878

G MINOR

Fanna I	Ricordi (Tomo)	Pincherle	Rinaldi
112	257	374	Op. 31, No. 14

PUBLICATIONS

Violin & Orchestra

Editor	Publisher	Series No.
Malipiero	G. Ricordi & Co.	PR 882

G MINOR

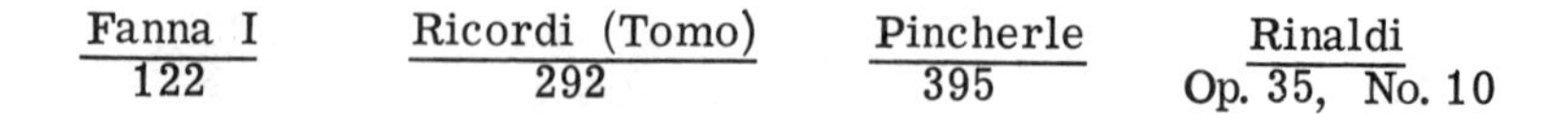

Fanna I	Ricordi (Tomo)	Pincherle	Rinaldi
122	292	395	Op. 35, No. 10

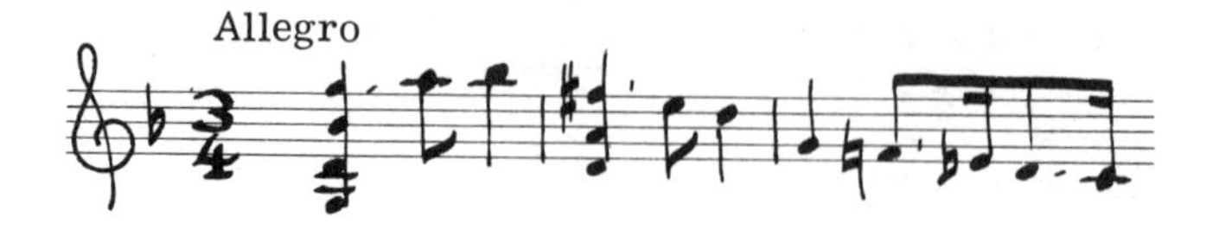

PUBLICATIONS

Violin & Orchestra

Editor	Publisher	Series No.
Malipiero	G. Ricordi & Co.	PR 942

G MINOR

Fanna I	Ricordi (Tomo)	Pincherle	Rinaldi
125	295	393	Op. 35, No. 2

PUBLICATIONS

Violin & Orchestra

Editor	Publisher	Series No.
Malipiero	G. Ricordi & Co.	PR 945

G MINOR

Fanna I	Ricordi (Tomo)	Pincherle	Rinaldi
147	329	352	

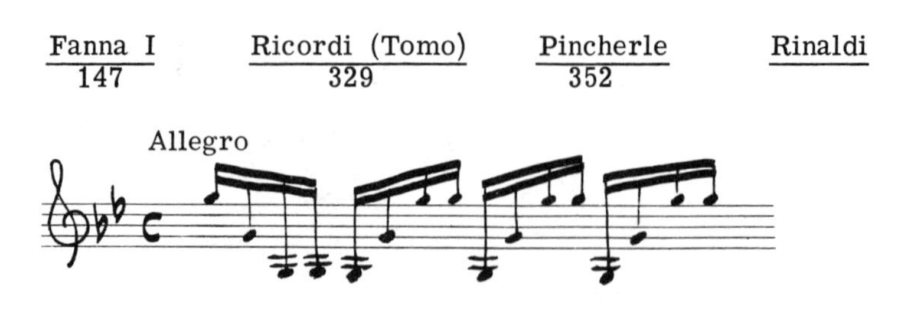

PUBLICATIONS

Violin & Orchestra

Editor	Publisher	Series No.
Malipiero	G. Ricordi & Co.	PR 979

G MINOR

Fanna I	Ricordi (Tomo)	Pincherle	Rinaldi
152	334	354	Op. 61, No. 18

PUBLICATIONS

Violin & Orchestra

Editor	Publisher	Series No.
Malipiero	G. Ricordi & Co.	PR 984

G MINOR

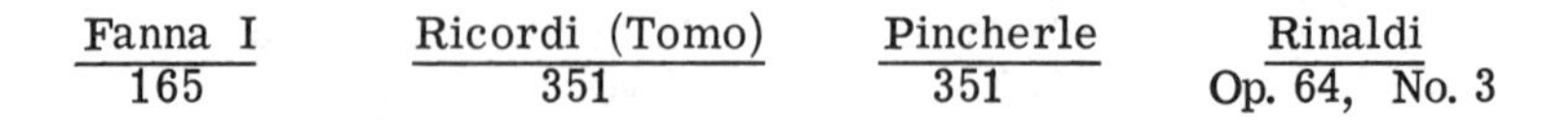

Fanna I	Ricordi (Tomo)	Pincherle	Rinaldi
165	351	351	Op. 64, No. 3

PUBLICATIONS

Violin & Orchestra

Editor	Publisher	Series No.
Malipiero	G. Ricordi & Co.	PR 1001

G MINOR

Fanna I	Ricordi (Tomo)	Pincherle	Rinaldi
185	423	328	Op. 4, No. 6

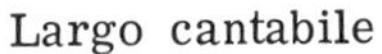

PUBLICATIONS

Violin & Orchestra

Editor	Publisher	Series No.
Ephrikian	G. Ricordi & Co.	PR 1098
Franko	Ries & Erler (C. F. Peters Corp. , U. S. agent)	

Violin & Piano

Editor	Publisher	Series No.
Franko	Ries & Erler (C. F. Peters Corp. , U. S. agent)	RE 2

RECORDINGS*

Label	Series No.
Bärenreiter	1832-2832

*See Appendix E

G MINOR

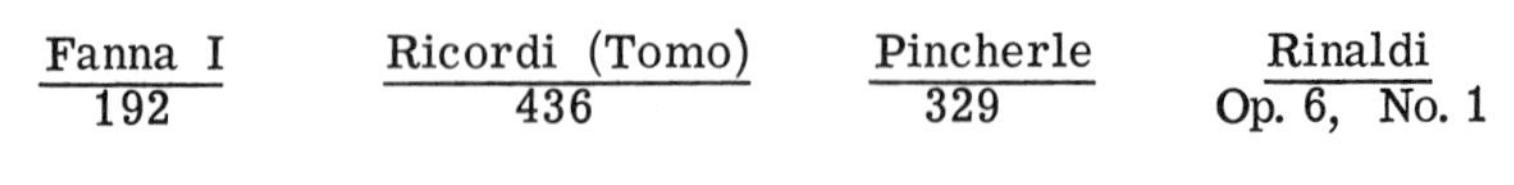

Fanna I	Ricordi (Tomo)	Pincherle	Rinaldi
192	436	329	Op. 6, No. 1

PUBLICATIONS

Violin & Orchestra

Editor	Publisher	Series No.
Malipiero	G. Ricordi & Co.	PR 1111
Gerheuser	Assoc. Music Pub.	
	Kalmus [for sale or rent]	
	Eulenburg [pocket score]	

G MINOR

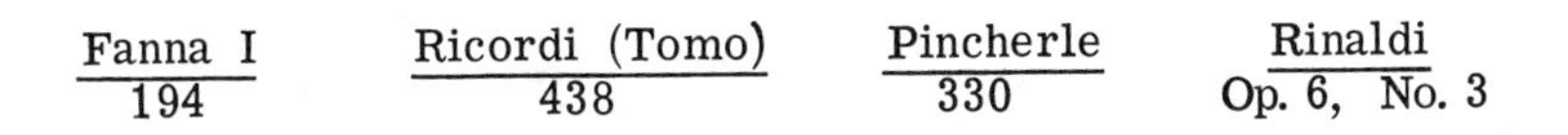

Fanna I	Ricordi (Tomo)	Pincherle	Rinaldi
194	438	330	Op. 6, No. 3

PUBLICATIONS

Violin & Orchestra

Editor	Publisher	Series No.
Malipiero	G. Ricordi & Co.	PR 1113

G MINOR

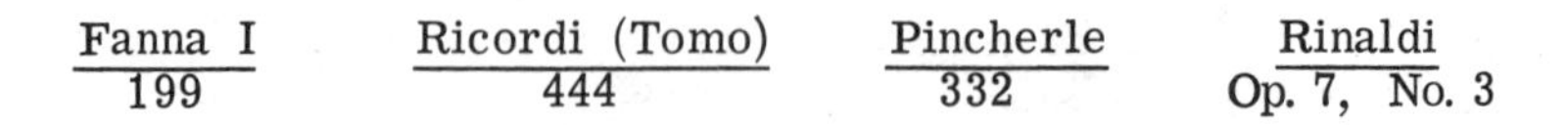

Fanna I	Ricordi (Tomo)	Pincherle	Rinaldi
199	444	332	Op. 7, No. 3

PUBLICATIONS

Violin & Orchestra

Editor	Publisher	Series No.
Malipiero	G. Ricordi & Co.	PR 1119

G MINOR

Fanna I	Ricordi (Tomo)	Pincherle	Rinaldi
211	462	343	Op. 12, No. 1

PUBLICATIONS

Violin & Orchestra

Editor	Publisher	Series No.
Malipiero	G. Ricordi & Co.	PR 1137
Nachez	Assoc. Music Pub.	
Kolneder	Assoc. Music Pub.	

Violin & Piano

Editor	Publisher	Series No.
Lenzewski	B. Schotts Söhne	3696
Nachez	B. Schotts Söhne (Assoc. Music Pub., U. S. agent)	901

RECORDINGS

Label	Series No.	Label	Series No.
Angel	35444	Monitor	2018
Bach	538	Vanguard	1059; 2073
Bruno	14019	Westminster	18718

Begin: Concertos in A Major

Fanna I	Ricordi (Tomo)	Pincherle	Rinaldi
5	16	236	Op. 31, No. 5 (Op. 56, No. 6)

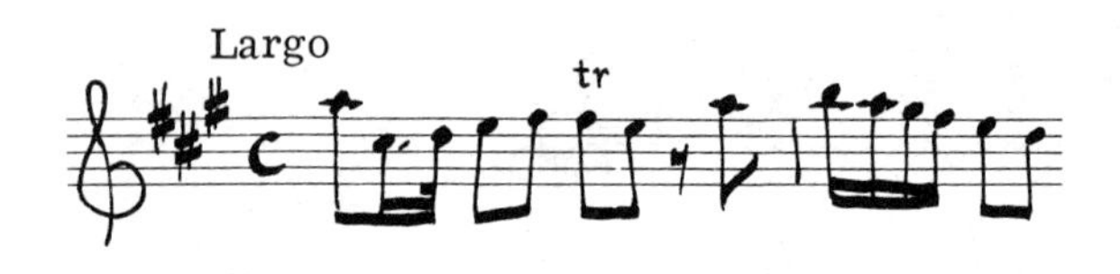

PUBLICATIONS

Violin & Orchestra

Editor	Publisher	Series No.
Maderna	G. Ricordi & Co.	PR 261

RECORDINGS

Label	Series No.
Angel	S-36001

A MAJOR

Scordatura

Fanna I	Ricordi (Tomo)	Pincherle	Rinaldi
39	100	229	Op. 20, No. 2

PUBLICATIONS

Violin & Orchestra

Editor	Publisher	Series No.
Malipiero	G. Ricordi & Co.	PR 462

RECORDINGS

Label	Series No.
Angel	S-36010

A MAJOR

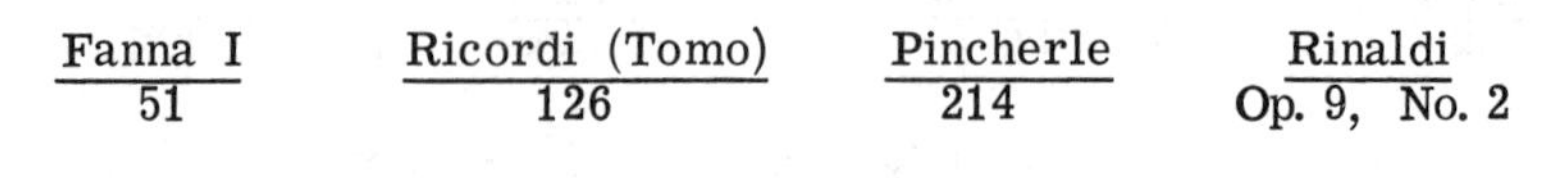

Fanna I	Ricordi (Tomo)	Pincherle	Rinaldi
51	126	214	Op. 9, No. 2

PUBLICATIONS

Violin & Orchestra

Editor	Publisher	Series No.
Malipiero	G. Ricordi & Co.	PR 576

RECORDINGS*

*See Appendix E

A MAJOR

(scordatura)

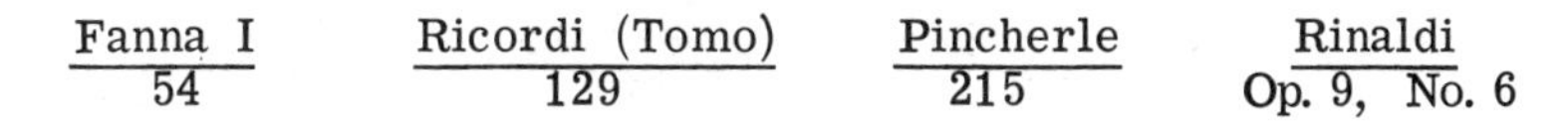

Fanna I	Ricordi (Tomo)	Pincherle	Rinaldi
54	129	215	Op. 9, No. 6

PUBLICATIONS

Violin & Orchestra

Editor	Publisher	Series No.
Malipiero	G. Ricordi & Co.	PR 579

RECORDINGS*

*See Appendix E

A MAJOR

Fanna I	Ricordi (Tomo)	Pincherle	Rinaldi
90	191	216	Op. 11, No. 3 (Op. 36, No. 18)

PUBLICATIONS

Violin & Orchestra

Editor	Publisher	Series No.
Malipiero	G. Ricordi & Co.	PR 716

A MAJOR

Fanna I	Ricordi (Tomo)	Pincherle	Rinaldi
104	229	237	Op. 31, No. 7

PUBLICATIONS

Violin & Orchestra

Editor	Publisher	Series No.
Malipiero	G. Ricordi & Co.	PR 829

Violin & Piano

Editor	Publisher	Series No.
Bellezza	G. Ricordi & Co.	129660

A MAJOR

Fanna I	Ricordi (Tomo)	Pincherle	Rinaldi
106	245	234	Op. 31, No. 3

PUBLICATIONS

Violin & Orchestra

Editor	Publisher	Series No.
Malipiero	G. Ricordi & Co.	PR 845

RECORDINGS

Label	Series No.
Angel	S-36001

A MAJOR

Fanna I	Ricordi (Tomo)	Pincherle	Rinaldi
123	293	225	Op. 35, No. 11

PUBLICATIONS

Violin & Orchestra

Editor	Publisher	Series No.
Malipiero	G. Ricordi & Co.	PR 943

A MAJOR

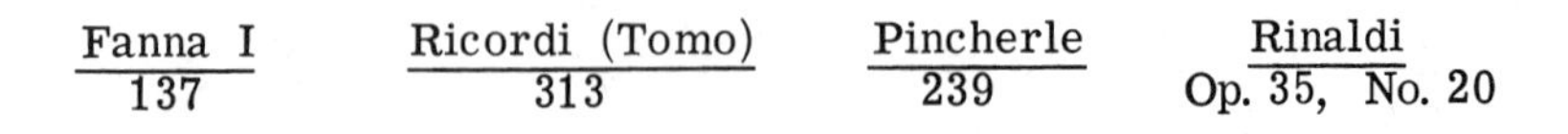

Fanna I	Ricordi (Tomo)	Pincherle	Rinaldi
137	313	239	Op. 35, No. 20

PUBLICATIONS

Violin & Orchestra

Editor	Publisher	Series No.
Malipiero	G. Ricordi & Co.	PR 963

A MAJOR

(per l' "eco in lontano")

Fanna I	Ricordi (Tomo)	Pincherle	Rinaldi
139	319	222	Op. 62, No. 2

PUBLICATIONS

Violin & Orchestra

Editor	Publisher	Series No.
Malipiero	G. Ricordi & Co.	PR 969

RECORDINGS

Label	Series No.
Deutsche Grammophon Gesellschaft	18947-138947
" " "	ARC-198318
" " "	ARC-3218;73218

A MAJOR

Fanna I	Ricordi (Tomo)	Pincherle	Rinaldi
141	323	228	

PUBLICATIONS

Violin & Orchestra

Editor	Publisher	Series No.
Malipiero	G. Ricordi & Co.	PR 973

RECORDINGS

Label	Series No.
Angel	36004;S-36004

A MAJOR

Fanna I	Ricordi (Tomo)	Pincherle	Rinaldi
148	230	227	

PUBLICATIONS

Violin & Orchestra

Editor	Publisher	Series No.
Malipiero	G. Ricordi & Co.	PR 980

A MAJOR

Fanna I	Ricordi (Tomo)	Pincherle	Rinaldi
155	339	223	

PUBLICATIONS

Violin & Orchestra

Editor	Publisher	Series No.
Malipiero	G. Ricordi & Co.	PR 989

A MAJOR

Concerto for 2 Violins

Fanna I	Ricordi (Tomo)	Pincherle	Rinaldi
159	344	224	Op. 62, No. 1

Allegro

Largo

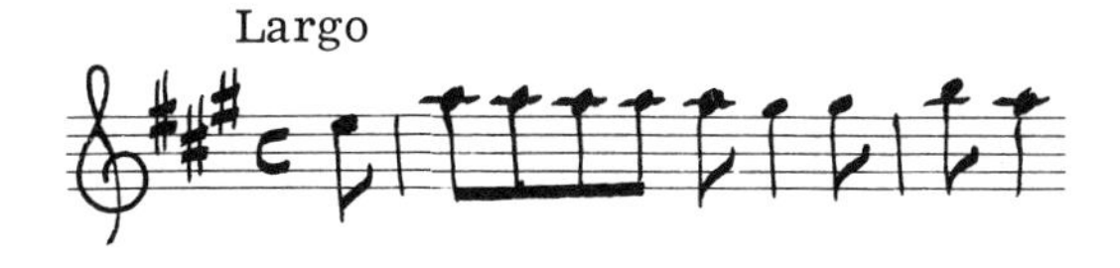

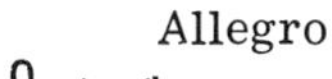

PUBLICATIONS

Violin & Orchestra

Editor	Publisher	Series No.
Malipiero	G. Ricordi & Co.	PR 994

A MAJOR

Concerto for 2 Violins

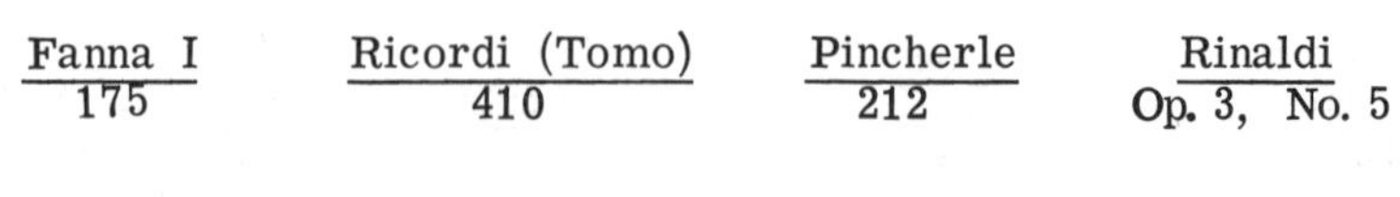

Fanna I	Ricordi (Tomo)	Pincherle	Rinaldi
175	410	212	Op. 3, No. 5

PUBLICATIONS

Violin & Orchestra

Editor	Publisher	Series No.
Malipiero	G. Ricordi & Co.	PR 1085

Violin & Piano

Editor	Publisher	Series No.
Füssl	Bärenreiter-Verlag	3713

RECORDINGS*

Label	Series No.
Angel	45030

*See Appendix E

A MAJOR

Fanna I	Ricordi (Tomo)	Pincherle	Rinaldi
184	422	213	Op. 4, No. 5

PUBLICATIONS

Violin & Orchestra

Editor	Publisher	Series No.
Ephrikian	G. Ricordi & Co.	PR 1097

RECORDINGS*

*See Appendix E

A MAJOR

Fanna I	Ricordi (Tomo)	Pincherle	Rinaldi
221	485	217	

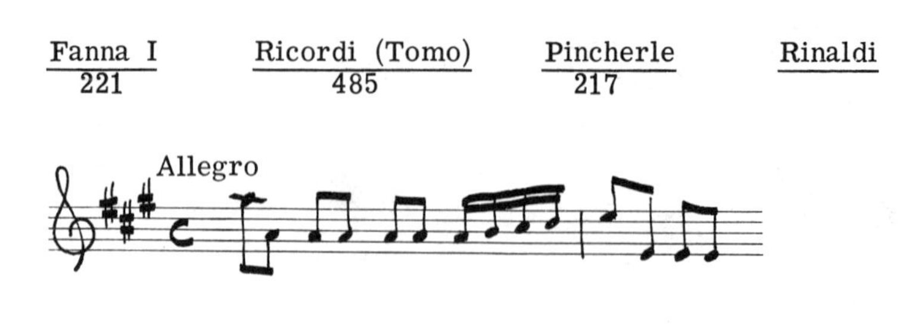

A MAJOR

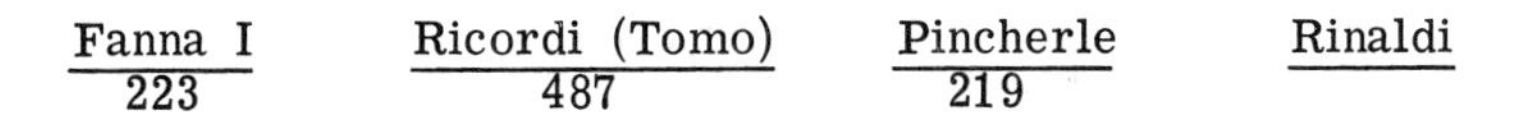

Fanna I	Ricordi (Tomo)	Pincherle	Rinaldi
223	487	219	

A MAJOR

Fanna I	Ricordi (Tomo)	Pincherle	Rinaldi
224	489	221	Op. 66

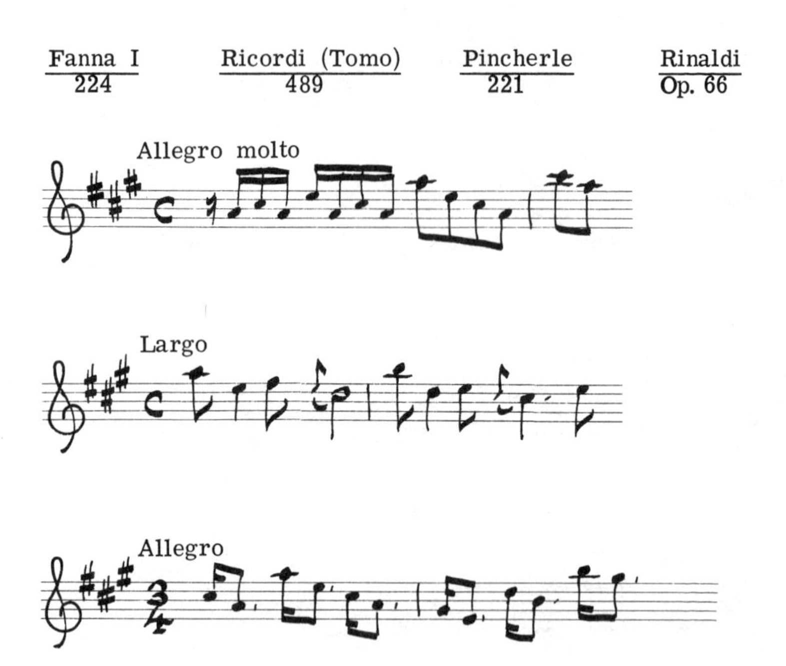

A MAJOR

Fanna I
227
Ricordi (Tomo)
496
Pincherle
232
Rinaldi
Allegro
Adagio
3
3
3
Allegro

Begin: Concertos in A Minor

Fanna I	Ricordi (Tomo)	Pincherle	Rinaldi
53	128	10	Op. 9, No. 5 Op. 61, No. 19

PUBLICATIONS

Violin & Orchestra

Editor	Publisher	Series No.
Malipiero	G. Ricordi & Co.	PR 578

RECORDINGS*

*See Appendix E

A MINOR

Concerto for 2 Violins

Fanna I	Ricordi (Tomo)	Pincherle	Rinaldi
61	140	28	Op. 58, No. 2

PUBLICATIONS

Violin & Orchestra

Editor	Publisher	Series No.
Malipiero	G. Ricordi & Co.	PR 590

RECORDINGS

Label	Series No.
Epic	SC-6040; BSC-111

A MINOR

Fanna I	Ricordi (Tomo)	Pincherle	Rinaldi
176	411	1	Op. 3, No. 6

PUBLICATIONS

Violin & Orchestra

Editor	Publisher	Series No.
Malipiero	G. Ricordi & Co.	PR 1086
Nachez	Assoc. Music Pub.	
	International Music Co. [for rent]	
	Eulenburg [pocket score] (C. F. Peters Corp., U. S. agent)	
Muller	Kjos Music Co. (3rd movt.)	01009

Violin & Piano

Editor	Publisher	Series No.
Abbado	G. Ricordi & Co.	130164
Borrell	Senart (Franco Colombo, U. S. agent)	5347
Galamian	International Music Co.	
Kuechler	C. F. Peters Corp.	3794
Nachez	B. Schotts Söhne (Assoc. Music Pub., U. S. agent)	
Perlman	Carl Fischer, Inc.	B-2631

RECORDINGS*

Label	Series No.
Bach	538
Bärenreiter	1832-2832
Nonesuch	1022;71022

*See Appendix E

A MINOR

Concerto for 2 Violins

Fanna I	Ricordi (Tomo)	Pincherle	Rinaldi
177	413	2	Op. 3, No. 8

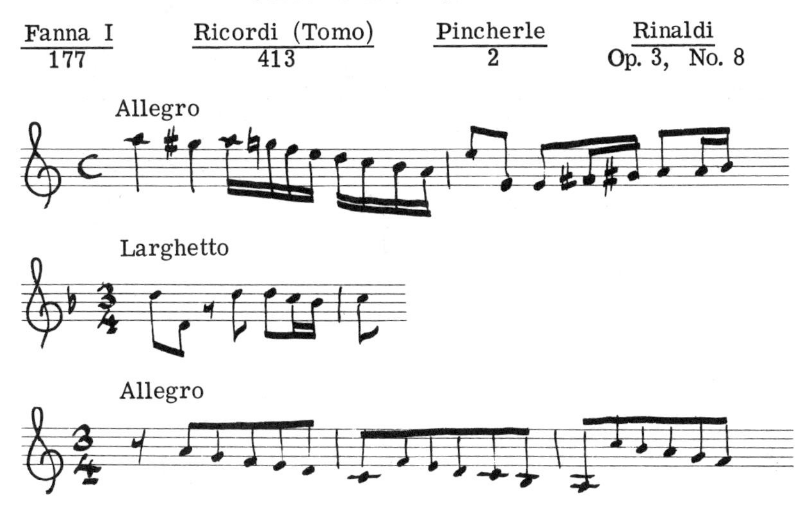

PUBLICATIONS

Violin & Orchestra

Editor	Publisher	Series No.
Malipiero	G. Ricordi & Co.	PR 1088
Einstein	Eulenburg [pocket score] (C. F. Peters Corp., U. S. agent)	4869
	Miniscore	762

Violin & Piano

Editor	Publisher	Series No.
Galamian	International Music Co.	
Vené	Franco Colombo, Inc.	2071

RECORDINGS*

Label	Series No.	Label	Series No.
Angel	36006;S-36006	Decca	9729
Amadee	6206	Decca	9950
Angelicum	5958	Deutsche Grammophon Gesellschaft	18714; 138714
Angelicum	5961-S-5161	Epic	LC-3565
Audio Fi	50036	Nonesuch	71022
Bruno	14019	Regent	5051
Columbia	ML-5087		

*See Appendix E

A MINOR

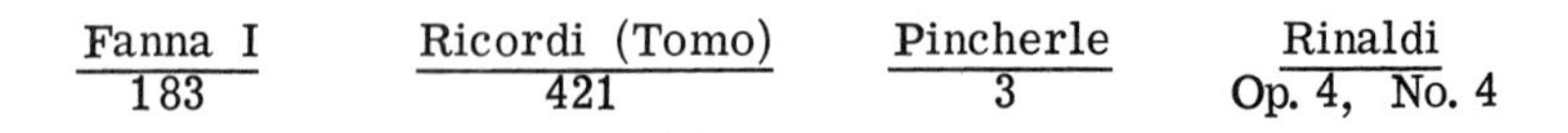

Fanna I	Ricordi (Tomo)	Pincherle	Rinaldi
183	421	3	Op. 4, No. 4

PUBLICATIONS

Violin & Orchestra

Editor	Publisher	Series No.
Ephrikian	G. Ricordi & Co.	PR 1096

RECORDINGS*

*See Appendix E

A MINOR

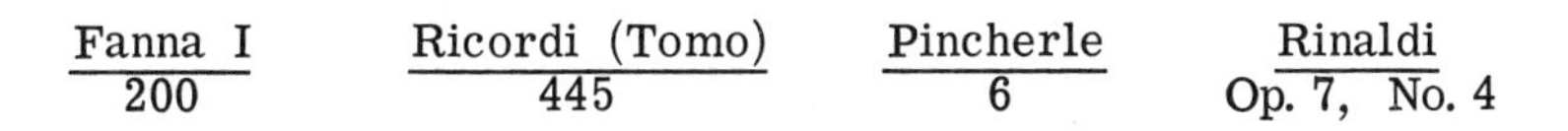

Fanna I	Ricordi (Tomo)	Pincherle	Rinaldi
200	445	6	Op. 7, No. 4

PUBLICATIONS

Violin & Orchestra

Editor	Publisher	Series No.
Malipiero	G. Ricordi & Co.	PR 1120

A MINOR

Fanna I	Ricordi (Tomo)	Pincherle	Rinaldi
236	519	92	

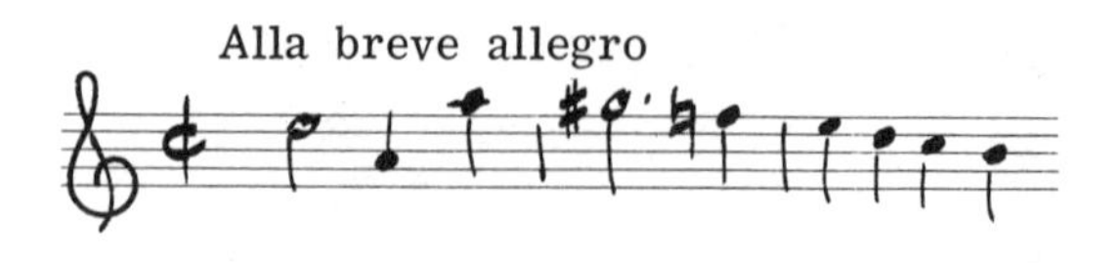

Begin: Concertos in B♭ Major

Fanna I	Ricordi (Tomo)	Pincherle	Rinaldi
1	1	405	Op. 33, No. 8

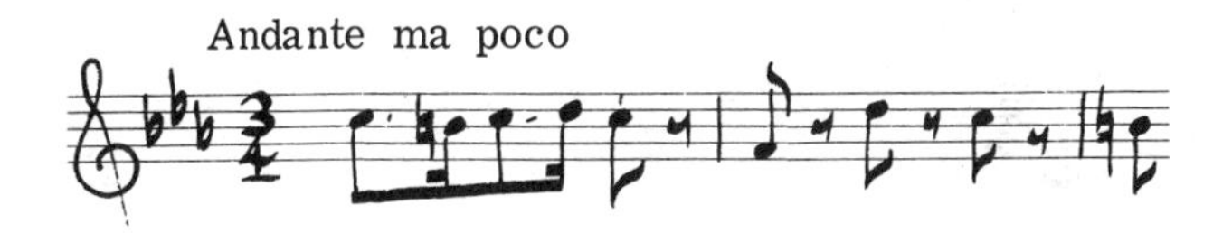

PUBLICATIONS

Violin & Orchestra

Editor	Publisher	Series No.
Ephrikian	G. Ricordi & Co.	PR 229

B♭ MAJOR

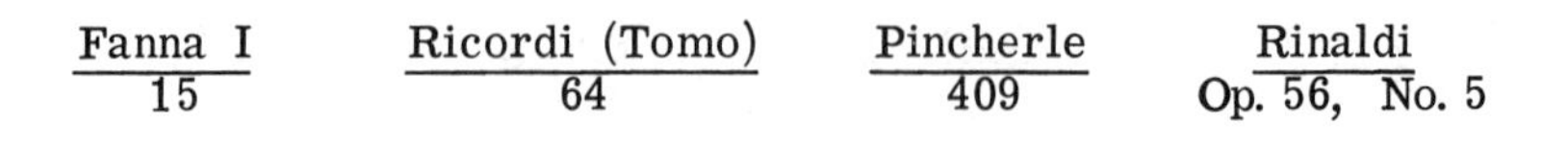

Fanna I	Ricordi (Tomo)	Pincherle	Rinaldi
15	64	409	Op. 56, No. 5

PUBLICATIONS

Violin & Orchestra

Editor	Publisher	Series No.
Malipiero	G. Ricordi & Co.	PR 351

B♭ MAJOR

"La Caccia"

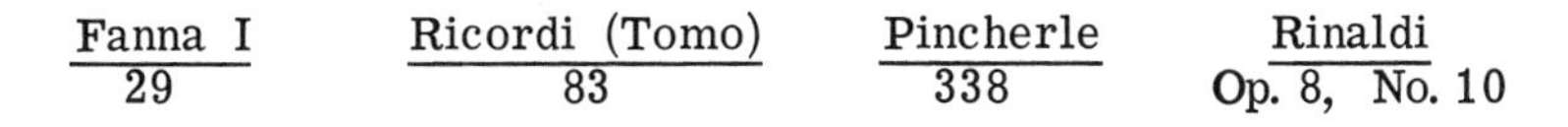

Fanna I	Ricordi (Tomo)	Pincherle	Rinaldi
29	83	338	Op. 8, No. 10

PUBLICATIONS

Violin & Orchestra

Editor	Publisher	Series No.
Malipiero	G. Ricordi & Co.	PR 445

RECORDINGS*

*See Appendix E

B♭ MAJOR

Fanna I	Ricordi (Tomo)	Pincherle	Rinaldi
32	86	373	Op. 31, No. 12

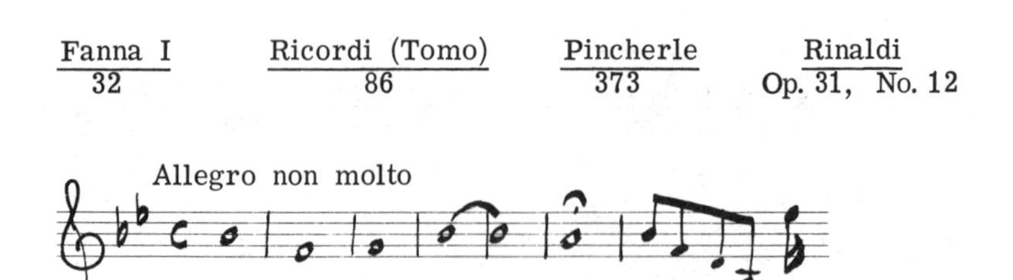

PUBLICATIONS

Violin & Orchestra

Editor	Publisher	Series No.
Malipiero	G. Ricordi & Co.	PR 448

B♭ MAJOR

Concerto for 2 Violins

Fanna I	Ricordi (Tomo)	Pincherle	Rinaldi
40	107	390	Op. 21, No. 5

PUBLICATIONS

Violin & Orchestra

Editor	Publisher	Series No.
Malipiero	G. Ricordi & Co.	PR 557

B♭ MAJOR

Concerto for 2 Violins

Fanna I	Ricordi (Tomo)	Pincherle	Rinaldi
42	111	391	Op. 21, No. 6

PUBLICATIONS

Violin & Orchestra

Editor	Publisher	Series No.
Malipiero	G. Ricordi & Co.	PR 561

B♭ MAJOR

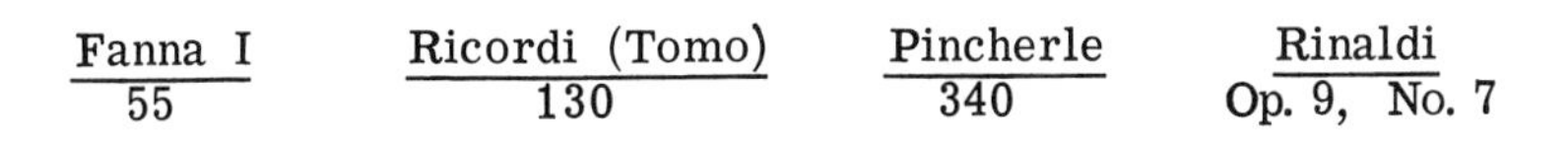

PUBLICATIONS

Violin & Orchestra

Editor	Publisher	Series No.
Malipiero	G. Ricordi & Co.	PR 580

RECORDINGS*

*See Appendix E

B♭ MAJOR

Concerto for 2 Violins

Fanna I	Ricordi (Tomo)	Pincherle	Rinaldi
57	132	341	Op. 9, No. 9

PUBLICATIONS

Violin & Orchestra

Editor	Publisher	Series No.
Malipiero	G. Ricordi & Co.	PR 582

RECORDINGS*

*See Appendix E

B♭ MAJOR

Concerto for 4 Violins

Fanna I	Ricordi (Tomo)	Pincherle	Rinaldi
59	134	367	Op. 27, No. 5

PUBLICATIONS

Violin & Orchestra

Editor	Publisher	Series No.
Malipiero	G. Ricordi & Co.	PR 584

RECORDINGS

Label	Series No.
C. B. S.	32110003;32110004

B♭ MAJOR

Concerto for Violin and 2 Orchestras
(scordatura)

Fanna I	Ricordi (Tomo)	Pincherle	Rinaldi
60	136	368	Op. 28, No. 3

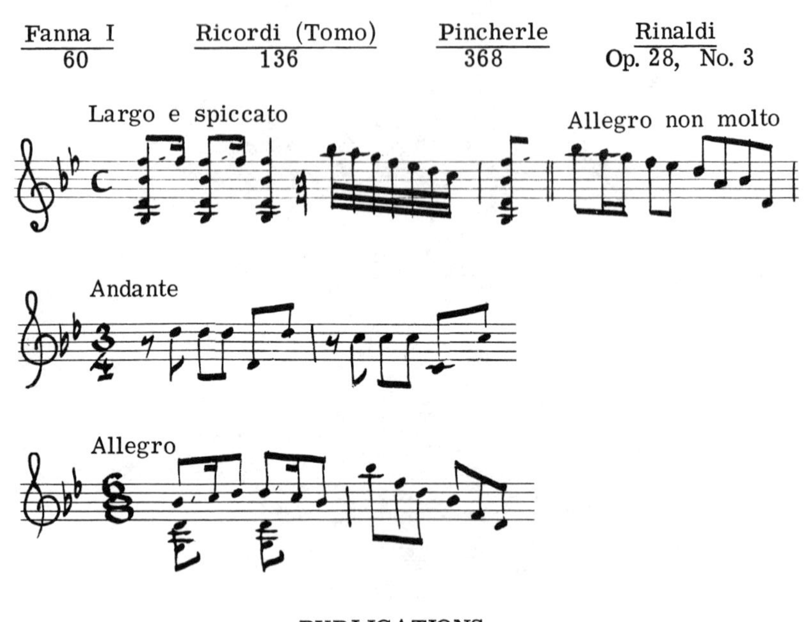

PUBLICATIONS

Violin & Orchestra

Editor	Publisher	Series No.
Malipiero	G. Ricordi & Co.	PR 586

RECORDINGS

Label	Series No.
Bach Guild	665;70665
Mercury	50401;90401
Seraphim	S-60118
Washington University	406;9406
Westminster	19123;17123

B♭ MAJOR

Concerto for 2 Violins

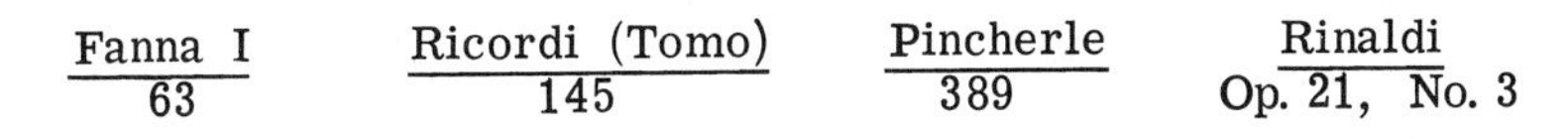

Fanna I	Ricordi (Tomo)	Pincherle	Rinaldi
63	145	389	Op. 21, No. 3

PUBLICATIONS

Violin & Orchestra

Editor	Publisher	Series No.
Malipiero	G. Ricordi & Co.	PR 595

B♭ MAJOR

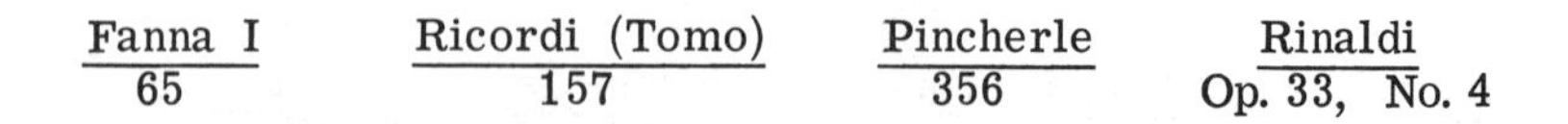

Fanna I	Ricordi (Tomo)	Pincherle	Rinaldi
65	157	356	Op. 33, No. 4

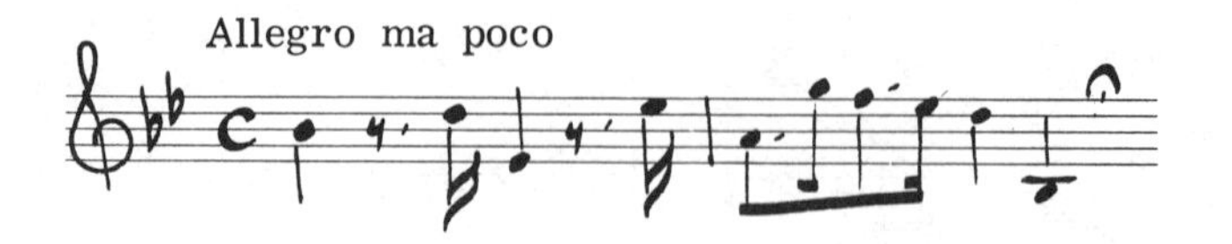

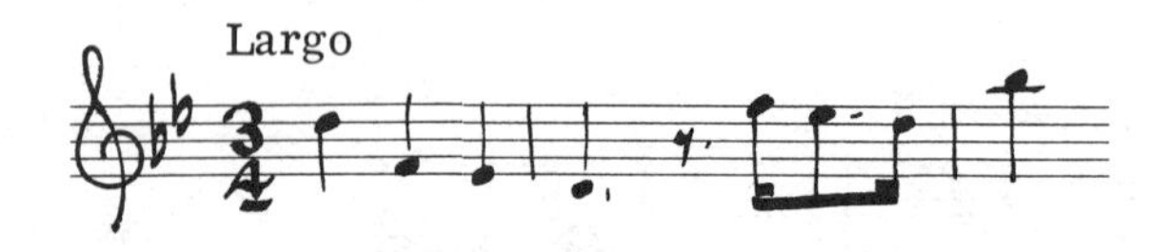

PUBLICATIONS

Violin & Orchestra

Editor	Publisher	Series No.
Malipiero	G. Ricordi & Co.	PR 682

B♭ MAJOR

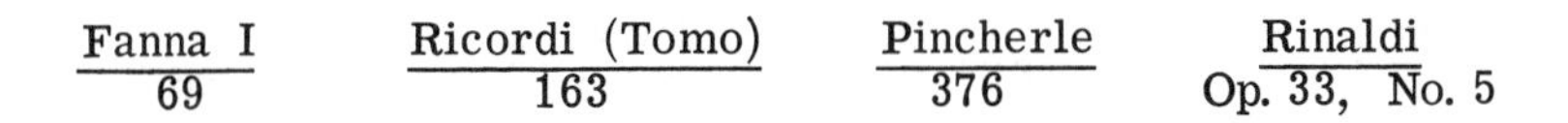

Fanna I	Ricordi (Tomo)	Pincherle	Rinaldi
69	163	376	Op. 33, No. 5

PUBLICATIONS

Violin & Orchestra

Editor	Publisher	Series No.
Malipiero	G. Ricordi & Co.	PR 688

B♭ MAJOR

Fanna I	Ricordi (Tomo)	Pincherle	Rinaldi
76	170	377	Op. 33, No. 15

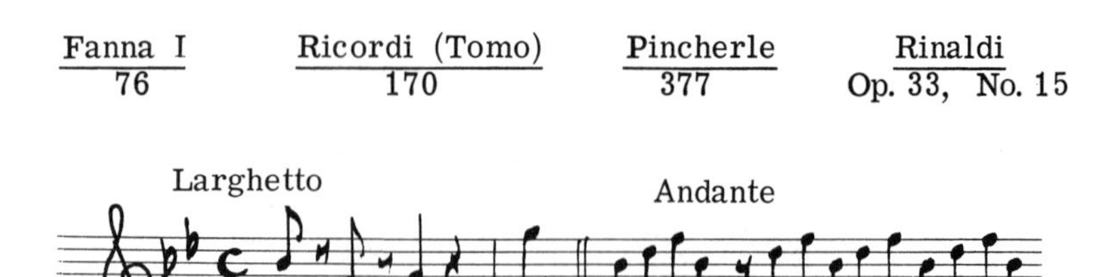

PUBLICATIONS

Violin & Orchestra

Editor	Publisher	Series No.
Malipiero	G. Ricordi & Co.	PR 695

B♭ MAJOR

Fanna I	Ricordi (Tomo)	Pincherle	Rinaldi
78	172	378	Op. 33, No. 18

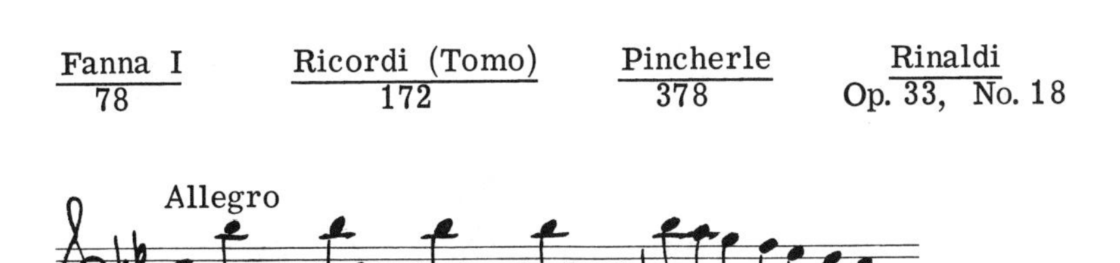

PUBLICATIONS

Violin & Orchestra

Editor	Publisher	Series No.
Malipiero	G. Ricordi & Co.	PR 697

B♭ MAJOR

Fanna I	Ricordi (Tomo)	Pincherle	Rinaldi
86	183	344	Op. 12, No. 5 (Op. 36, No. 9)

PUBLICATIONS

Violin & Orchestra

Editor	Publisher	Series No.
Malipiero	G. Ricordi & Co.	PR 708

B♭ MAJOR

Fanna I	Ricordi (Tomo)	Pincherle	Rinaldi
95	199	349	Op. 36, No. 11

PUBLICATIONS

Violin & Orchestra

Editor	Publisher	Series No.
Malipiero	G. Ricordi & Co.	PR 724

B♭ MAJOR

Concerto for 2 Violins

Fanna I	Ricordi (Tomo)	Pincherle	Rinaldi
99	208	365	Op. 27, No. 1

PUBLICATIONS

Violin & Orchestra

Editor	Publisher	Series No.
Malipiero	G. Ricordi & Co.	PR 758

B♭ MAJOR

Fanna I	Ricordi (Tomo)	Pincherle	Rinaldi
117	262	375	Op. 31, No. 19

PUBLICATIONS

Violin & Orchestra

Editor	Publisher	Series No.
Malipiero	G. Ricordi & Co.	PR 887

B♭ MAJOR

Fanna I	Ricordi (Tomo)	Pincherle	Rinaldi
118	284	370	Op. 31, No. 1

PUBLICATIONS

Violin & Orchestra

Editor	Publisher	Series No.
Malipiero	G. Ricordi & Co.	PR 934

B♭ MAJOR

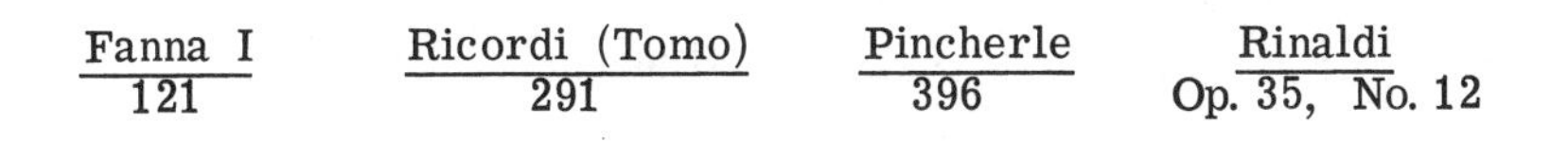

Fanna I	Ricordi (Tomo)	Pincherle	Rinaldi
121	291	396	Op. 35, No. 12

PUBLICATIONS

Violin & Orchestra

Editor	Publisher	Series No.
Malipiero	G. Ricordi & Co.	PR 941

B♭ MAJOR

Fanna I	Ricordi (Tomo)	Pincherle	Rinaldi
150	332	358	

PUBLICATIONS

Violin & Orchestra

Editor	Publisher	Series No.
Malipiero	G. Ricordi & Co.	PR 982

B♭ MAJOR

"O sia Corneto da Posta"

Fanna I	Ricordi (Tomo)	Pincherle	Rinaldi
163	348	350	

PUBLICATIONS

Violin & Orchestra

Editor	Publisher	Series No.
Malipiero	G. Ricordi & Co.	PR 998

RECORDINGS

Label	Series No.
Westminster	19123-17123

B♭ MAJOR

Fanna I	Ricordi (Tomo)	Pincherle	Rinaldi
170	377	353	

Allegro

Largo e cantabile

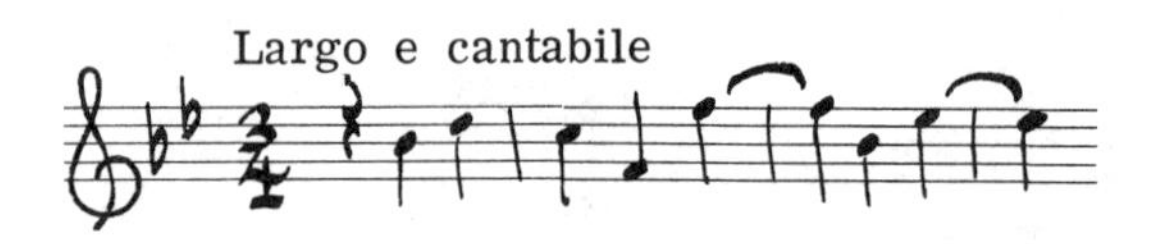

Allegro

PUBLICATIONS

Violin & Orchestra

Editor	Publisher	Series No.
Malipiero	G. Ricordi & Co.	PR 1052

B♭ MAJOR

Fanna I	Ricordi (Tomo)	Pincherle	Rinaldi
180 (235 1st movt. only)	418	327	Op. 4, No. 1

PUBLICATIONS

Violin & Orchestra

Editor	Publisher	Series No.
Ephrikian	G. Ricordi & Co.	PR 1093
Frenkel	Ries & Erler (C. F. Peters Corp., U. S. agent)	
	Bärenreiter-Verlag	356
	Kalmus [for sale or rent]	

Violin & Piano

Editor	Publisher	Series No.
Frenkel	Ries & Erler (C. F. Peters Corp., U. S. agent)	RE 114

RECORDINGS*

*See Appendix E

B♭ MAJOR

Fanna I	Ricordi (Tomo)	Pincherle	Rinaldi
202	447	333	Op. 7, No. 6

Allegro

Largo

Allegro

PUBLICATIONS

Violin & Orchestra

Editor	Publisher	Series No.
Malipiero	G. Ricordi & Co.	PR 1122

B♭ MAJOR

Fanna I	Ricordi (Tomo)	Pincherle	Rinaldi
204	450	335	Op. 7, No. 9

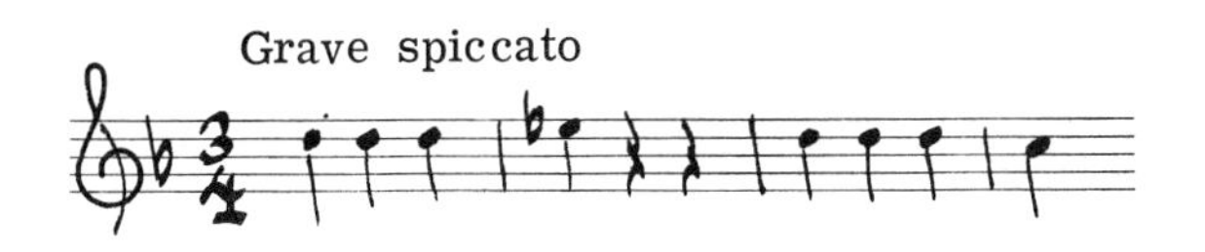

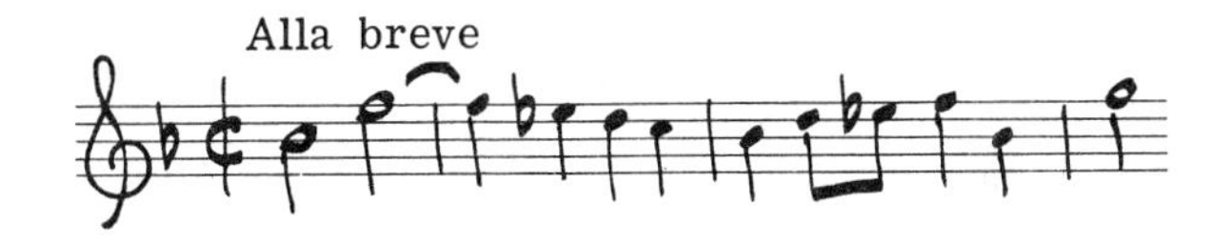

PUBLICATIONS

Violin & Orchestra

Editor	Publisher	Series No.
Malipiero	G. Ricordi & Co.	PR 1125

B♭ MAJOR

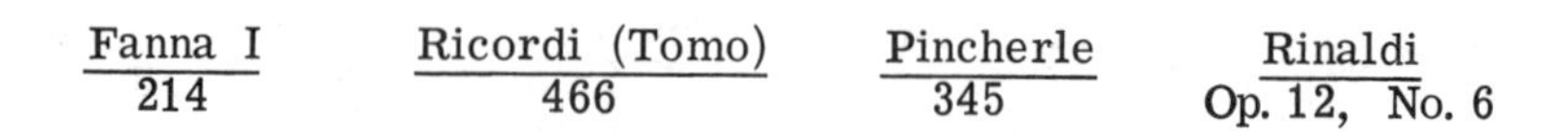

Fanna I	Ricordi (Tomo)	Pincherle	Rinaldi
214	466	345	Op. 12, No. 6

PUBLICATIONS

Violin & Orchestra

Editor	Publisher	Series No.
Ephrikian	G. Ricordi & Co.	PR 1141

B♭ MAJOR

Fanna I	Ricordi (Tomo)	Pincherle	Rinaldi
219	483	346	Op. 16, No. 1

B♭ MAJOR

Fanna I	Ricordi (Tomo)	Pincherle	Rinaldi
230	499	364	

B♭ MAJOR

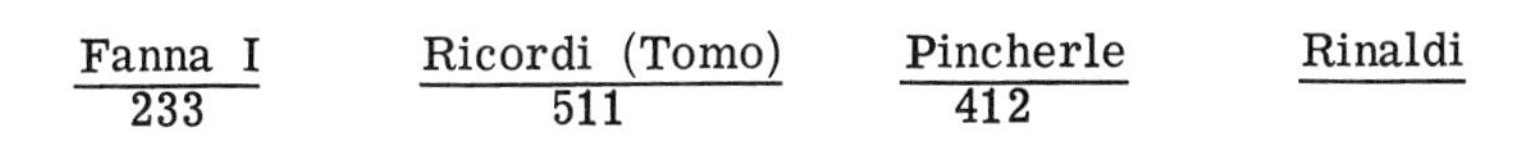

Fanna I	Ricordi (Tomo)	Pincherle	Rinaldi
233	511	412	

B♭ MAJOR

Fanna I	Ricordi (Tomo)	Pincherle	Rinaldi
235 (180 1st movt. only)	514	327	Op. 4, No. 1 (1st movt. only)

Begin: Concertos in B Minor

Fanna I	Ricordi (Tomo)	Pincherle	Rinaldi
38	96	184	Op. 33, No. 6

PUBLICATIONS

Violin & Orchestra

Editor	Publisher	Series No.
Malipiero	G. Ricordi & Co.	PR 458

B MINOR

(scordatura)

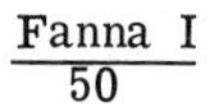

Fanna I	Ricordi (Tomo)	Pincherle	Rinaldi
50	125	154	Op. 9, No. 12

PUBLICATIONS

Violin & Orchestra

Editor	Publisher	Series No.
Malipiero	G. Ricordi & Co.	PR 575
Carmirelli	Edizioni Zanibon (C. F. Peters Corp., U. S. agent)	

RECORDINGS*

*See Appendix E

B MINOR

Fanna I	Ricordi (Tomo)	Pincherle	Rinaldi
77	171	185	Op. 33, No. 12

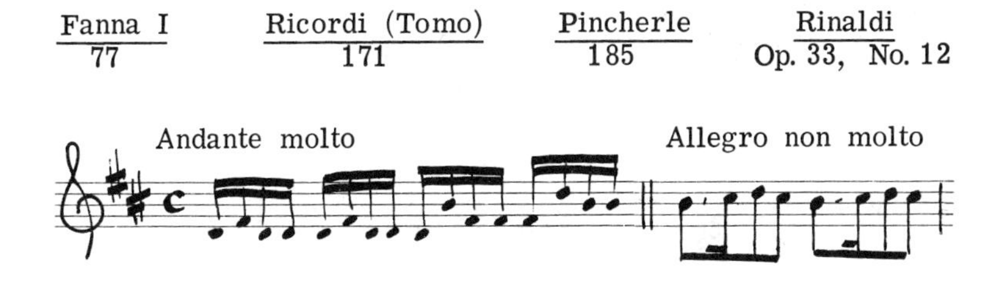

PUBLICATIONS

Violin & Orchestra

Editor	Publisher	Series No.
Malipiero	G. Ricordi & Co.	PR 696

B MINOR

Fanna I	Ricordi (Tomo)	Pincherle	Rinaldi
83	179	202	Op. 36, No. 7

PUBLICATIONS

Violin & Orchestra

Editor	Publisher	Series No.
Malipiero	G. Ricordi & Co.	PR 704

B MINOR

Fanna I	Ricordi (Tomo)	Pincherle	Rinaldi
115	260	183	Op. 31, No. 18

PUBLICATIONS

Violin & Orchestra

Editor	Publisher	Series No.
Malipiero	G. Ricordi & Co.	PR 885

B MINOR

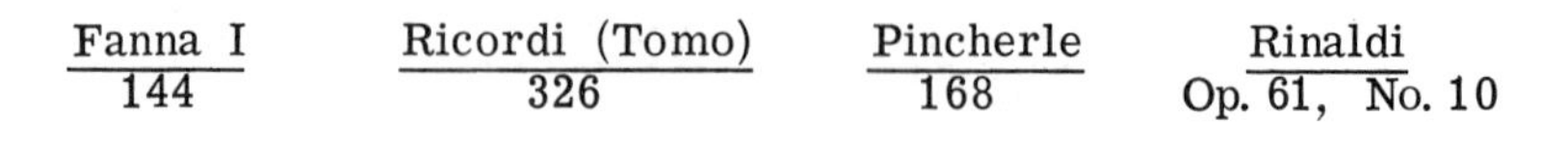

Fanna I	Ricordi (Tomo)	Pincherle	Rinaldi
144	326	168	Op. 61, No. 10

PUBLICATIONS

Violin & Orchestra

Editor	Publisher	Series No.
Malipiero	G. Ricordi & Co.	PR 976

B MINOR

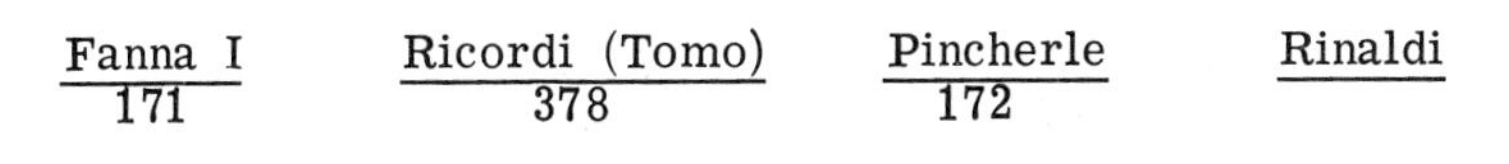

Fanna I	Ricordi (Tomo)	Pincherle	Rinaldi
171	378	172	

PUBLICATIONS

Violin & Orchestra

Editor	Publisher	Series No.
Malipiero	G. Ricordi & Co.	PR 1053

B MINOR

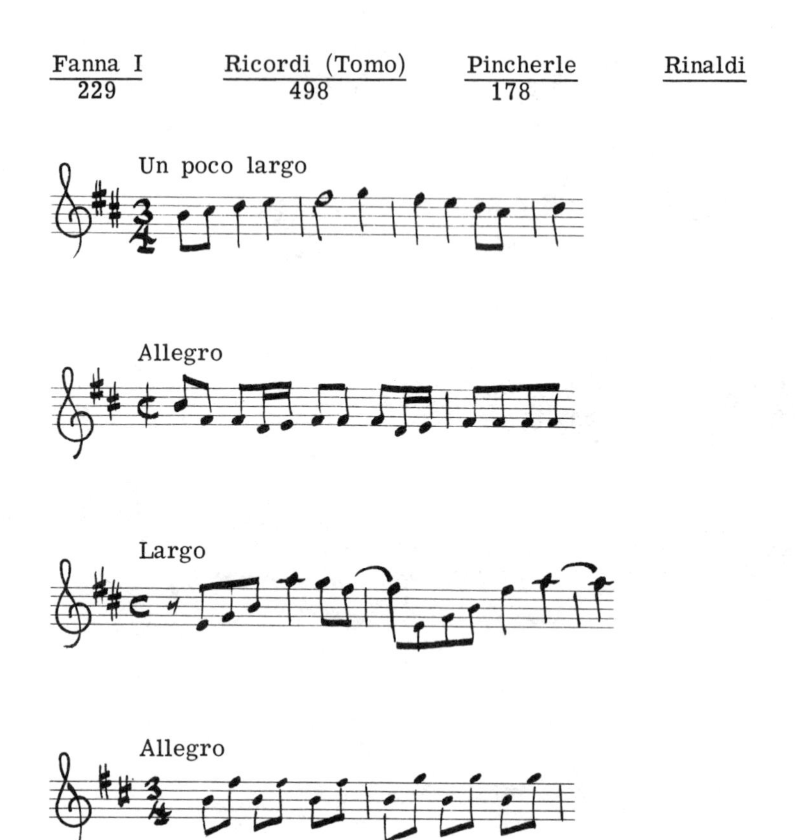
Fanna I
229
Ricordi (Tomo)
498
Pincherle
178
Rinaldi
Un poco largo
Allegro
Largo
Allegro

Chapter III

SUGGESTIONS FOR HANDBOOK USE AND FURTHER RESEARCH

It is hoped that this Handbook will be useful to musicians and non-musicians alike. If it has simplified the matter of locating and identifying Vivaldi's violin concertos, this guide will have served its purpose.

It is suggested that the reader become familiar with all of the Appendices. Frequently a concerto will be listed by a number from one of the three catalog systems, and it will save valuable time to look up the given number in its separate Appendix listing, and then find the page where this particular work is located in the incipit guide (Chapter II).

There are numerous publications of Vivaldi's concertos which it has been impossible to list here largely because they are listed only by key classification. Probably most of these are concertos which are classified in this Handbook, but procuring the music or recording would be very difficult, time-consuming, and expensive for the researcher. Those concertos which are known only by key will eventually be identified through the matching of themes, and possibly they may be added to this Handbook as they are discovered by the user. It is for this reason that each concerto was listed in the incipit guide on a separate page. Additional information can then be listed, whenever it becomes available.

One encounters many unexpected problems when compiling a handbook of this nature. The selection of a suitable incipit for each movement can sometimes be a very difficult decision to make, especially when several melodic voices appear together. The incipits used in this Handbook were determined by selecting the most important melodic voice which appeared in the first few measures of a movement.

A heavy responsibility also falls upon the researcher when he attempts to select the best edition or manuscript to use as his musical source. Editions vary as to quality, and many times the matter is further complicated, as in Vivaldi's case, where the composer has written several manuscripts for the same work, each being slightly different from the others.

Considering that Vivaldi wrote over 530 instrumental works, one is not surprised to find duplications of some themes and even of complete movements. The writer in this Handbook has attempted to indicate in the incipit guide if a particular movement recurs in some other works.

Many suggested areas for further research come to mind as one becomes familiar with Vivaldi's violin music. The unusual key relationship among movements, in many of the concertos, makes one inquisitive as to whether there are any recurring patterns in the selection of keys used within a concerto.

The form structure of the concertos is unique in many instances, and it would be interesting to discover whether Vivaldi's concertos became solidified over the years into a fairly standardized form, or whether he used novel and experimental ideas throughout the bulk of them.

Teachers should be interested in classifying the concertos as to the level of difficulty. These concertos range from the lower intermediate to the most difficult virtuoso level.

In closing, it is hoped that these suggestions may encourage others to begin to explore the scores of these works, and possibly initiate an interest in bringing them back into the performance repertoire.

APPENDICES

(Guided to Page Numbers in Chapter II)

Appendix A. Key List in Chromatic Scale Order

Appendix B. Fanna I Numbers of Ricordi

Fanna	Incipit on page	Fanna	Incipit on page
1	221	39	195
2	52	40	225
3	24	41	66
4	125	42	226
5	194	43	28
6	161	44	29
7	126	45	67
8	60	46	30
9	112	47	31
10	61	48	128
11	97	49	162
12	53	50	254
13	25	51	196
14	54	52	178
15	222	53	214
16	176	54	197
17	144	55	227
18	62	56	100
19	63	57	228
20	145	58	55
21	98	59	229
22	127	60	230
23	177	61	215
24	146	62	68
25	160	63	231
26	113	64	163
27	26	65	232
28	99	66	149
29	223	67	32
30	64	68	33
31	27	69	233
32	224	70	135
33	147	71	150
34	148	72	129
35	65	73	34
36	177b	74	136
37	134	75	114
38	253	76	234

Fanna	Incipit on page	Fanna	Incipit on page
77	255	122	184
78	235	123	201
79	56	124	74
80	69	125	185
81	179	126	104
82	180	127	131
83	256	128	152
84	130	129	75
85	35	130	153
86	236	131	119
87	164	132	76
88	151	133	77
89	70	134	78
90	198	135	40
91	165	136	79
92	115	137	202
93	36	138	80
94	37	139	203
95	237	140	41
96	166	141	204
97	71	142	105
98	181	143	106
99	238	144	258
100	101	145	132
101	116	146	42
102	117	147	186
103	167	148	205
104	199	149	81
105	57	150	242
106	200	151	107
107	168	152	187
108	182	153	82
109	118	154	108
110	169	155	206
111	38	156	120
112	183	157	43
113	102	158	83
114	39	159	207
115	257	160	84
116	72	161	154
117	239	162	85
118	240	163	243
119	103	164	121
120	73	165	188
121	241	166	122

Fanna	Incipit on page
167	155
168	170
169	44
170	244
171	259
172	45
173	171
174	137
175	208
176	216
177	217
178	86
179	133
180	245
181	138
182	172
183	218
184	209
185	189
186	46
187	109
188	156
189	58
190	87
191	173
192	190
193	123
194	191
195	88
196	139
197	110
198	47
199	192
200	219
201	157
202	246
203	174
204	247
205	158
206	89
207	90
208	140
209	175
210	59
211	193
212	111
213	48
214	248
215	159
216	141
217	49
218	91
219	249
220	142
221	210
222	92
223	211
224	212
225	93
226	50
227	213
228	94
229	260
230	250
231	124
232	51
233	251
234	95
235	252
236	220
237	96
238	143

Appendix C. Pincherle Numbers

Pincherle	Incipit on page	Pincherle	Incipit on page
1	216	101	139
2	217	102	174
3	218	103	162
4	46	106	140
5	47	107	175
6	219	108	141
7	26	109	142
8	27	111	165
9	31	112	170
10	214	117	166
11	48	121	167
12	49	122	168
14	25	124	169
17	29	125	135
18	43	126	136
19	41	132	161
20	45	136	164
20s (Sinfonia)	33	138	163
21	32	144	134
22	42	147	86
23	28	149	87
28	215	150	88
29	44	151	80&89
38	38	152	90
39	39	153	64
40	34	154	254
59	30	156	70
62	40	158	91
65	35	159	92
66	36	161	83
68	37	162	84
88	24	163	85
92	220	164	68
93	51	165	79
96	171	167	82
97	137	168	258
98	138	170	75
99	172	171	67
100	173	172	259

Pincherle	Incipit on page	Pincherle	Incipit on page
173	81	243	132
174	93	244	126
177	94	245	129
178	260	246	131
179	71	247	130
182	72	248	125
183	257	251	156
184	253	252	159
185	255	253	109
186	69	254	110
189	66	255	157
190	65	256	158
192	74	257	146
193	73	258	99
194	76	260	100
195	77	263	111
196	78	269	105
199	60	270	108
200	62	271	155
201	63	272	103
202	256	275	154
208	61	276	107
211	95	277	106
212	208	278	148
213	209	281	101
214	196	290	145
215	197	293	102
216	198	295	149
217	210	296	150
219	211	310	97
221	212	312	104
222	203	314	152
223	206	315	153
224	207	316	98
225	201	317	151
227	205	324	144
228	204	325	147
229	195	327	245
232	213	328	189
234	200	329	190
236	194	330	191
237	199	332	192
239	202	333	246
240	133	335	247
241	127	336	177
242	128	337	176

Pincherle	Incipit on page
338	223
339	178
340	227
341	228
343	193
344	236
345	248
346	249
349	237
350	243
351	188
352	186
353	244
354	187
355	123
356	232
357	180
358	242
364	250
365	238
366	181
367	229
368	230
370	240
372	182
373	224
374	183
375	239
376	233
377	234
378	235
379	179
389	231
390	225
391	226
393	185
395	184
396	241
405	221
408	177b
409	222
412	251
413	58
414	123
415	113
416	55

Pincherle	Incipit on page
417	59
418	121
419	52
420	120
421	122
423	116
425	117
426	57
428	118
429	112
430	114
431	56
435	54
436	53
437	119
439	115
442	160

Appendix D. Rinaldi Listing

Opus 3: "L'Estro Armonico"

Rinaldi	Incipit on Page
Op. 3 No. 3	171
Op. 3 No. 4	137
Op. 3 No. 5	208
Op. 3 No. 6	216
Op. 3 No. 8	217
Op. 3 No. 9	86
Op. 3 No. 12	133

Opus 4: "La Stravaganza"

Rinaldi	Incipit on Page
Op. 4 No. 1	245
Op. 4 No. 2	138
Op. 4 No. 3	172
Op. 4 No. 4	218
Op. 4 No. 5	209
Op. 4 No. 6	189
Op. 4 No. 7	46
Op. 4 No. 8	109
Op. 4 No. 9	156
Op. 4 No. 10	58
Op. 4 No. 11	87
Op. 4 No. 12	173

Opus 6

Rinaldi	Incipit on Page
Op. 6 No. 1	190
Op. 6 No. 2	123
Op. 6 No. 3	191
Op. 6 No. 4	88
Op. 6 No. 5	139
Op. 6 No. 6	110

Opus 7

Rinaldi	Incipit on Page
Op. 7 No. 2	47
Op. 7 No. 3	192
Op. 7 No. 4	219
Op. 7 No. 5	157
Op. 7 No. 6	246
Op. 7 No. 8	174
Op. 7 No. 9	247
Op. 7 No. 10	158
Op. 7 No. 11	89
Op. 7 No. 12	90

Opus 8: "Il Cimente dell' Armonia e dell'Invenzione ("The Four Seasons" Opus 8 Nos. 1-4)

Rinaldi	Incipit on Page
Op. 8 No. 1	127
Op. 8 No. 2	177
Op. 8 No. 3	146
Op. 8 No. 4	160
Op. 8 No. 5	113
Op. 8 No. 6	26
Op. 8 No. 7	99
Op. 8 No. 8	176
Op. 8 No. 10	223
Op. 8 No. 11	64
Op. 8 No. 12	27

Opus 9 "La Cetra"

Rinaldi	Incipit on Page
Op. 9 No. 1	31
Op. 9 No. 2	196
Op. 9 No. 3	178
Op. 9 No. 4	128
Op. 9 No. 5	214
Op. 9 No. 6	197
Op. 9 No. 7	227
Op. 9 No. 8	100
Op. 9 No. 9	228
Op. 9 No. 10	162
Op. 9 No. 11	55
Op. 9 No. 12	254

Rinaldi	Incipit on Page

Opus 11

Op. 11 No. 1	70
Op. 11 No. 2	140
Op. 11 No. 3	198
Op. 11 No. 4	175
Op. 11 No. 5	59
Op. 11 No. 6	178

Opus 12

Op. 12 No. 1	193
Op. 12 No. 2	111
Op. 12 No. 4	48
Op. 12 No. 5	236
Op. 12 No. 6	248

Opus 16

Op. 16 No. 1	249
Op. 16 No. 2	142

Opus 20

Op. 20 No. 1	97
Op. 20 No. 2	195

Opus 21 (Concertos for 2 Violins)

Op. 21 No. 1	161
Op. 21 No. 2	54
Op. 21 No. 3	231
Op. 21 No. 4	53
Op. 21 No. 5	225
Op. 21 No. 6	226
Op. 21 No. 7	66
Op. 21 No. 8	65
Op. 21 No. 9	29

Opus 23 (No. 1) (Concerto for 3 Violins)

Op. 23 No. 1	148

Rinaldi	Incipit on Page

Opus 27 (Concertos for 2 Violins, except No. 5)

Op. 27 No. 1	238
Op. 27 No. 2	181
Op. 27 No. 3	101
Op. 27 No. 4	116
Op. 27 No. 5 (for 4 Violins)	229

Opus 28

Op. 28 No. 1	166
Op. 28 No. 2	71
Op. 28 No. 3	230

Opus 31

Op. 31 No. 1	240
Op. 31 No. 2	145
Op. 31 No. 3	200
Op. 31 No. 4	167
Op. 31 No. 5	194
Op. 31 No. 6	117
Op. 31 No. 7	199
Op. 31 No. 8	57
Op. 31 No. 9	168
Op. 31 No. 10	182
Op. 31 No. 11	169
Op. 31 No. 12	224
Op. 31 No. 13	38
Op. 31 No. 14	183
Op. 31 No. 15	72
Op. 31 No. 16	102
Op. 31 No. 17	128
Op. 31 No. 18	257
Op. 31 No. 19	239
Op. 31 No. 20	39
Op. 31 No. 21	118

Op. 32 (No. 2 only)	33

Opus 33

Op. 33 No. 1	112

Rinaldi	Incipit on Page
Op. 33 No. 2	32
Op. 33 No. 3	149
Op. 33 No. 4	232
Op. 33 No. 5	233
Op. 33 No. 6	253
Op. 33 No. 7	135
Op. 33 No. 8	221
Op. 33 No. 9	150
Op. 33 No. 10	129
Op. 33 No. 11	34
Op. 33 No. 12	255
Op. 33 No. 13	136
Op. 33 No. 14	126
Op. 33 No. 15	234
Op. 33 No. 16	114
Op. 33 No. 17	69
Op. 33 No. 18	235
Op. 33 No. 19	179
Op. 33 No. 20	56

Opus 35

Rinaldi	Incipit on Page
Op. 35 No. 1	30
Op. 35 No. 2	185
Op. 35 No. 3	74
Op. 35 No. 4	103
Op. 35 No. 5	104
Op. 35 No. 6	131
Op. 35 No. 7	31
Op. 35 No. 8	73
Op. 35 No. 10	184
Op. 35 No. 11	201
Op. 35 No. 12	241
Op. 35 No. 13	80
Op. 35 No. 14	75
Op. 35 No. 15	152
Op. 35 No. 16	40
Op. 35 No. 17	153
Op. 35 No. 18	119
Op. 35 No. 19	79
Op. 35 No. 20	202
Op. 35 No. 21	76
Op. 35 No. 22	77
Op. 35 No. 23	78

Opus 36

Rinaldi	Incipit on Page
Op. 36 No. 1	176
Op. 36 No. 2	67
Op. 36 No. 3	98
Op. 36 No. 4	62
Op. 36 No. 5	180
Op. 36 No. 6	63
Op. 36 No. 7	256
Op. 36 No. 8	151
Op. 36 No. 9	236
Op. 36 No. 10	70
Op. 36 No. 11	237
Op. 36 No. 12	64
Op. 36 No. 13	130
Op. 36 No. 15	36
Op. 36 No. 16	164
Op. 36 No. 17	165
Op. 36 No. 18	198
Op. 36 No. 19	37
Op. 36 No. 20	115
Op. 37 (No. 1)	35
Op. 38 (No. 5 only)	60
Op. 47 (No. 1)	163

Opus 51

Rinaldi	Incipit on Page
Op. 51 No. 1	61
Op. 51 No. 2	125
Op. 51 No. 3	52

Opus 54

Rinaldi	Incipit on Page
Op. 54 No. 2	68
Op. 54 No. 3	25

Opus 56

Rinaldi	Incipit on Page
Op. 56 No. 1	144
Op. 56 No. 2	177b
Op. 56 No. 3	147

Rinaldi	Incipit on Page
Op. 56 No. 4	134
Op. 56 No. 5	222
Op. 56 No. 6	195
Op. 56 No. 7	24
Opus 58	
Op. 58 No. 1	28
Op. 58 No. 2	215
Opus 61	
Op. 61 No. 1	41
Op. 61 No. 2	106
Op. 61 No. 3	105
Op. 61 No. 4	83
Op. 61 No. 5	84
Op. 61 No. 6	85
Op. 61 No. 7	165
Op. 61 No. 8	45
Op. 61 No. 9	108
Op. 61 No. 10	258
Op. 61 No. 11	120
Op. 61 No. 12	158
Op. 61 No. 13	28
Op. 61 No. 14	122
Op. 61 No. 15	55
Op. 61 No. 16	154
Op. 61 No. 17	75
Op. 61 No. 18	187
Op. 61 No. 19	214
Op. 61 No. 20	148
Opus 62	
Op. 62 No. 1	207
Op. 62 No. 2	203
Op. 64 (No. 3 only)	188
Opus 66	212

Appendix E. Record Album Collections of Vivaldi Violin Concertos

Opus 3: "L'Estro Armonico"

Label	Series No.
Bach Guild	572/4
Bach Guild	5016/8
Decca	10070/2;710070
DGG Archives	198449
Odeon	ALP-1809/11;ASD-391/3
Phillips	WS-PHC-3-017
Qualiton	1095/7
Vanguard	SRV-143/5;SRV-143SSD
Vox	PL-7423
Vox	VEX 20

Opus 4: "La Stravaganza"

Label	Series No.
Phillips	2-940
Turnabout	4040;34040
Vox	DL-103
Vox	VBX-31;SVBX-531

Opus 8: "Il Cimente dell'Armonia e dell'Invenzione"

Label	Series No.
Angel	3611-c;S-3611-c (35877/9;S-35877/9)
Epic	SC-6029
Vox	DL-173
Westminster	3515(L-8913/5)

(Opus 8, Nos. 1-4) "The Four Seasons"

Label	Series No.
Angel	35216
Angel	35877;S-35877

(Opus 8, Nos. 1-4 con't.)

Label	Series No.
Angelicum	5949
Audio Fidelity	50032
Bach Guild	564
Bach Guild	5001
Boston	400
Cet.	Cet-50004
Columbia	ML-5044
Columbia	ML-5595; MS-6195
Columbia	ML-6144; MS-6744
Con.	CHC-1
Con.	RG-120
Decca	9423;79423
DGG Archive	3141-73141
DGG Archive	198641
Electrecord	90099;S-90099
Epic	BC-1086
Epic	LC-3216
Epic	LC-3704
Kapp	9056;S-9056
London	LLP-386
London	LL-3070
London	6044;21013
Mercury	14041;18041
Music Guild	S-177
Nonesuch	1070;71070
Odyssey	321-60132
Period	SHO-2309;SHOST-2309
Phillips	WS-9104
Qualiton	1102;S-1102
RCA Victor	LM-2424; LSC-2424
RCA Victor (Ital.)	MS-20026
Richmond	19056
Turnabout	34040
Vics	1469
Vox	9520
Vox	11480; 511480st
Westminster	14087

(Excerpts from Opus 8)

Label	Series No.
RCA Victor (Nos. 5-8)	LM-2743; LSC-2743

(Excerpts from Opus 8 con't.)

Label	Series No.
Epic (Nos. 5-12)	LC-3443
Con. (Nos. 5-12)	CHS-1064

Opus 9: "La Cetra"

Label	Series No.
Bach Guild	607/9;5033/5
Con.	CHS-1134
Epic	SC-6029
Phillips	PHM-3-595; PHS-3-993
Vox	173
Vox	DL-203
Vox	VBX-30

(Excerpts from Opus 9)

Label	Series No.
Epic (Nos. 9-12)	SC-6029
Vanguard (Nos. 4, 8, 9, 12)	SRV-159:SRV-1595

BIBLIOGRAPHY

Coral, Lenore. A Concordance of the Thematic Indexes to the Instrumental Works of Antonio Vivaldi. Ann Arbor: Music Library Association Publication, 1965.

Farish, Margaret K. String Music in Print. New York: R. R. Bowker, 1965.

Farish, Margaret K. Supplement to String Music in Print. New York: R. R. Bowker, 1968.

Long Playing Record Catalog (Monthly Guide to Stereo Records). Boston: W. Schwann, Inc., 1949-1970.

Pincherle, Marc. Antonio Vivaldi et la Musique Instrumentale, Tomo 2: Inventaire Thèmatique. Paris: Librarie Floury, 1948.

Ricordi Istitute Italiano Antonio Vivaldi. Catalogo Numerico Tematico delle Opere Strumentale. Italy: G. Ricordi, 1968.

Rinaldi, Mario. Numerico Tematico dello Composizioni di Antonio Vivaldi. Italy: Editrice Culture Moderna, 1945.

Vivaldi, Antonio. Le Opere de Antonio Vivaldi. Rome: Edizioni Ricordi, 1947.